AMERICA IN THE 1940s

CHARLES A. WILLS

Facts On File, Inc.

A Stonesong Press Book
Decades of American History: *America in the 1940s*

Copyright © 2006 by Stonesong Press, LLC

Facts On File, Inc.
132 West 31st Street
New York NY 10001

Library of Congress Cataloging-in-Publication Data

Wills, Charles.
   America in the 1940s / Charles A. Wills.
        p. cm.—(Decades of American history)
   "A Stonesong Press book."
   Includes bibliographical references and index.
   ISBN 0-8160-5639-0
  1. United States—History—1933–1945—Juvenile literature. 2. United
States—History—1945–1953—Juvenile literature. 3. Nineteen
forties—Juvenile literature.   I. Title. II. Series.
   E806.W475 2005
   973.918—dc22

                                                                2004018950

Facts On File books are available at special discounts when purchased in bulk quantities
for businesses, associations, institutions, or sales promotions. Please call our Special Sales
Department in New York at (212) 967-8800 or (800) 322-8755.

You can find Facts On File on the World Wide Web at http://www.factsonfile.com

Text design by Laura Smyth, Smythetype
Photo research by Larry Schwartz
Cover design by Pehrsson Design

Printed in the United States of America

VB PKG 10 9 8 7 6 5 4 3 2 1

This book is printed on acid-free paper.

CONTENTS

CHAPTER 1

THE UNITED STATES IN 1940

ABOUT 132 MILLION PEOPLE LIVED IN the United States as the 1940s began. There were 48 stars on the flag. Alaska and Hawaii were still territories. New York was the most populous state, with more than 13.5 million people. Nevada, the least populous state, had just 110,000 inhabitants. California was fifth, with 5.7 million residents.

Half of all Americans lived in the northeastern part of the country—the area north of the Potomac and Ohio rivers and east of the Mississippi River. A little more than half of the country's population lived in towns and cities. New York City was the nation's biggest, with about 7.5 million people. Chicago came in second, with about 3.4 million.

President Franklin Roosevelt appears on the cover of *Look* magazine, in a photo taken in Warm Springs, Georgia, in 1939. Roosevelt's calm and confident leadership helped the nation endure years of economic depression and world war. *(Library of Congress)*

Students read their textbooks in a high school classroom in Harrison, New York, in 1940. In that year, for the first time, half of the young adults in the United States finished high school. *(Library of Congress)*

According to the census of 1940, almost 90 percent of Americans were of European ancestry, and a little less than 10 percent of the population was African American. Native Americans and Asian Americans together accounted for less than one-half of 1 percent of the population. At this time the census did not count Americans of Hispanic ancestry separately, but the number of Hispanic Americans certainly increased in the decades before 1940, as immigrants from Mexico began moved into states such as Texas and California.

A large majority of Americans in 1940 considered themselves Christian. Most people belonged to various Protestant denominations, but Roman Catholics formed the single largest religious group. The Jewish population was about 5 million.

Americans in 1940 were better educated than in previous years. All but about 5 percent of Americans could read and write. Federal laws outlawing child labor and state laws requiring school attendance meant that more children went to school and stayed in school longer. The year 1940 was the first in which half of all young Americans finished high school. Only about one in 10 Americans, however, had a college degree in 1940, and only about one in four high-school graduates went on to college.

Most Americans in the 1940s were born in the United States, another big change from earlier decades. In 1920, almost half of all Americans had been born overseas, or had at least one parent who was foreign-born. In the 1920s, however, Congress passed laws that greatly restricted immigration. In the 1930s, only about 50,000 immigrants arrived in the country each year, in contrast to the 1 million who immigrated each year in the early 1900s.

Thanks to advances in health care, Americans were living longer. About 10 percent of Americans were 60

On May 15, 1940, the first practical heliopter, the Sikorsky VS-300, made a successful test flight outside Hartford, Connecticut, with its inventor—Russian-born engineer Igor Sikorsky—at the controls.

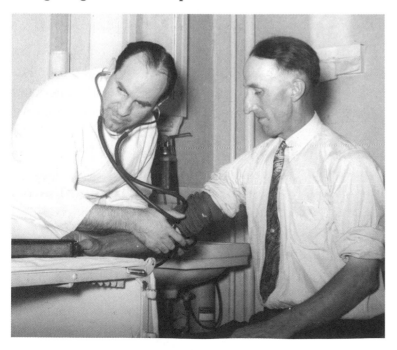

A doctor with the federal Farm Security Administration (FSA) checks a farmer's blood pressure. *(Library of Congress)*

HATTIE McDANIEL

Singer and actress Hattie McDaniel made movie history in 1940 when she became the first African-American performer to win an Academy Award. McDaniel was selected as Best Supporting Actress for her role in *Gone With the Wind.* When the movie was released in 1939, however, McDaniel could not attend the premiere, because it was held in segregated Atlanta, Georgia.

Besides her movie work, Hattie McDaniel had a recording career as a singer in the 1920s, and she starred in a popular radio program from 1947 to 1951. *(Private Collection)*

years of age or older in 1940. The population was still relatively young, however. About one in four Americans in 1940 was 15 years of age or younger, and about half of all Americans were under 30 years of age.

In the 1920s and 1930s, developments such as national radio networks, chain stores, and movies helped reduce the differences from region to region, which created a more national culture. Even so, the daily lives of Americans in various parts of the country remained very different. The South, in particular, lagged behind the rest of the country in many areas, including education.

The United States of 1940 was also a nation deeply divided along racial lines. African Americans, especially those living in the southern states, faced a lack of opportunity in jobs and education. In many southern states, laws denied African Americans their civil and political rights, including the right to vote and to serve on juries.

The South also had a system of segregation. In the segregated South, African Americans could not ride in the same train cars as whites, eat in the same restaurants, stay in the same hotels, or shop in the same stores. The 1894 U.S. Supreme Court case that legalized segregation, *Plessy v. Ferguson,* said that public facilities for whites and African Americans could be separate, though they had to be equal. In practice, they rarely were. Public accomodations for African Americans were usually inferior.

Starting around World War I, many African Americans responded to the lack of opportunities by moving from the rural South to the industrial cities of the Northeast and Midwest—a move known as the Great Migration, which continued through the 1920s and 1930s. By 1940, about half of all African Americans lived outside the South. Even in the northern cities, however, African Americans faced widespread prejudice in jobs, education, and housing.

Signs like this one were a common sight in the southern states during the 1940s. *(Library of Congress)*

Daily life for many Americans in 1940 was less comfortable than life is for Americans today. For example, in 1940 scarcely more than half of all U.S. homes had hot and cold running water, bathtubs, and indoor toilets. About 90 percent of homes in towns and cities had electricity, but only a third of the nation's farms did.

A DECADE OF DEPRESSION

In 1940, Americans were still living through one of the most difficult times in the nation's history. This era was known as the Great Depression—an economic crisis that led millions of people to lose their jobs, their savings, and their homes.

The 1920s had been a prosperous time for many Americans. There were plenty of jobs. Paychecks got bigger, and there was plenty to spend them on. More and more Americans owned their own homes and

African-American track-and-field athlete Jesse Owens won four gold medals at the 1936 Olympic Games in Berlin, Germany— humiliating Germany's racist Nazi regime.

WHAT'S UP, DOC?

In July 1940, the Warner Brothers movie studio released its first cartoon, *A Wild Hair.* The short film was the first outing for a wisecracking rabbit named Bugs Bunny. Tex Avery, Bugs's creator, based the character on movie comedian Groucho Marx. Mel Blanc provided Bugs's voice, along with those of the other classic Warner Brothers cartoon characters.

A frustrated Elmer Fudd confronts his prey in one of Warner Brothers immensely popular Looney Toons cartoons. *(Private Collection)*

THE GRAPES OF WRATH

The 1940 Pulitzer Prize for fiction went to John Steinbeck for his novel *The Grapes of Wrath.* The book told the story of the Joads, a family that leaves its dust-bound Oklahoma farm and makes a desperate journey to California in search of a better life, only to find disappointment and injustice. Director John Ford's movie version, starring Henry Fonda as Tom Joad, also appeared in 1940. The book inspired a song written by the great folksinger Woody Guthrie.

The Joads leave their Oklahoma farm for California in this scene from director John Ford's movie version of *The Grapes of Wrath.* *(Private Collection)*

bought cars and other goods. Some people invested their money in the stock market, which rose higher every year. By the end of the decade, some people thought the good times would go on forever.

The good times ended suddenly in October 1929. Stock prices on the New York Stock Exchange fell, wiping out the gains of the previous years and leaving many investors bankrupt. The crash of the stock exchange sent shock waves throughout the U.S. economy. Factories closed their doors, and banks and businesses failed.

By 1931, as many as one in four U.S. workers had no job. In some hard-hit cities, the jobless figure was much higher. Even workers who still had jobs faced pay cuts and short-ened hours. Many people could not continue paying their rent or mort-gage payments, and they became homeless. Hundreds of thousands of people roamed the streets and high-ways in search of a job—any job.

Outside of the cities, the depres-sion was even worse in many places. Before the 1929 crash, farmers could get only low prices for their crops. The depression lowered crop prices even further. Then nature seemed to turn against the farmers. A period of drought, or low rainfall, and high winds created the dust bowl in much of the Southwest and Midwest. Millions of tons of soil blew away, forming dust clouds that sometimes blotted out the sun.

Many rural Americans abandoned their dust-choked farms and headed west, hoping for a job pick-ing fruits and vegetables on the vast farms of California. Oklahoma, one of the states hit hardest by the dust bowl, lost 60,000 people between 1930 and 1940. Those who made it to California usually found nothing but backbreaking work that hardly paid enough to feed their families.

In this time of fear and uncertainty, a new presi-dent took office. He was Franklin Delano Roosevelt, a Democrat, who defeated the incumbent Republican president Herbert Hoover in 1932. When Roosevelt took office, he told Americans that "the only thing we have to fear is fear itself." He pledged "a New Deal" for Americans. He became popular and was often known by his initials, FDR.

During the depression, hundreds of thousands of hungry, desperate Americans left their homes in search of any kind of work. The couple shown here are migrant fruit pickers in Michigan. *(Library of Congress)*

"First of all, let me assert my firm belief that the only thing we have to fear is fear itself."

—Franklin Roosevelt's first Inaugural Address, March 4, 1933

The 1939 Pulitzer Prize for fiction went to Marjorie Kinnan Rawlings for *The Yearling*, a novel about a Florida boy and his pet deer. The book remains a beloved classic today.

Roosevelt quickly set about making the New Deal program a reality. He took swift steps to prop up the nation's failing banks. He increased the amount of federal funds available to help the hungry and homeless. He created new government agencies, such as the Public Works Administration (PWA), Work Projects Administration (WPA), and the Civilian Conservation Corps (CCC), which put jobless people to work building bridges, roads, dams, and other public works.

Not everyone agreed with Roosevelt's New Deal. Some Americans felt that the federal government was becoming too powerful and was interfering too much with private businesses. The New Deal, however, helped the people suffering the worst effects of the depression, and Roosevelt's confidence gave hope to a nation in crisis. The president won a second term in 1936, defeating Republican challenger Alf Landon in a landslide victory.

Despite Roosevelt's efforts, the depression hung on. By the end of the 1930s, the worst was over, but about 8 million Americans were still jobless, and factory production was still well below what it had been before October 1929.

This photograph shows one of the huge dust storms that ravaged much of the country during the 1930s. *(Library of Congress)*

Two workers pour concrete for a Civilian Conservation Corps (CCC) project. The CCC provided jobs for more than 500,000 young men between 1933 and 1942. *(Library of Congress)*

"*Brother, Can You Spare a Dime?*"

—Depression lament turned into a popular song by lyricist Yip Harburg

STORM CLOUDS OVER EUROPE

By 1940, Americans were worried not only about events at home but also overseas. The years after World War I were a time of fear and uncertainty in much of the world. Several ruthless dictators took advantage of these circumstances to rise to power.

Several years after the Bolshevik Revolution in 1917, a Communist takeover, Russia became the Soviet Union. By the 1930s the nation was under the iron rule of Joseph Stalin. In Germany, the National Socialist Party, also known as the Nazi Party, under the leadership of Adolf Hitler, came to power in 1933. Benito Mussolini's National Fascist Party already ruled Italy. Throughout the 1930s, democratically elected governments in many smaller European countries were replaced by dictatorships, too. By the end of the decade, France and Great Britain were the only major European countries with democratic governments.

Although many people considered the Soviet Union the greatest threat to peace in Europe, it was Nazi Germany that made the first move toward war with its neighbors. Hitler, whose Nazi Party proclaimed

In 1936, the Baseball Writers' Association of America (BBWAA) voted in the first five members of the Baseball Hall of Fame—Ty Cobb, Babe Ruth, Honus Wagner, Christy Matthewson, and Walter Johnson.

Soviet dictator Joseph Stalin ruled for 25 years. Millions of Soviet citizens were executed or died in prison camps during Stalin's brutal reign. *(Library of Congress)*

"This will strike like a bomb... Now Europe is mine."

—Adolf Hitler after the signing of the German-Soviet Non-Aggression Pact

the superiority of the German people and considered Jews and several other groups to be subhuman, built up Germany's military forces, in violation of the Versailles Treaty that set the peace terms immediately after World War I. When Hitler united Germany and Austria and began demanding territory from surrounding countries, Britain and France protested but did not take military action.

In 1938, Hitler demanded that Czechoslovakia (today the nations of Slovakia and the Czech Republic) give Germany the Sudetenland, a Czech region where many German-speaking people lived. In order to keep the peace, Britain and France persuaded the Czech government to give the Sudetenland to Germany. Hitler, in return, agreed not to demand any more Czech territory. A year later he broke his promise and occupied all of Czechoslovakia.

Britain and France now realized the danger of trying to make deals with Hitler, but it was too late. In August 1939, the world was stunned to learn that Germany and the Soviet Union had signed a Non-Aggression Pact—a treaty in which each nation pledged not to attack each other. Nazi Germany and the Soviet Union had been bitter enemies; now they were friends.

On September 1, German troops invaded Poland, and France and Britain declared war on Germany. For the second time in a quarter-century, Europe was at war. Soviet forces invaded Poland a few weeks later. Poland was quickly defeated and the country was divided up between Germany and the Soviet Union.

NEUTRALITY AND ISOLATIONISM

Three days after the German invasion of Poland, President Roosevelt declared that the United States would be neutral in the European conflict. A majority of Americans approved of Roosevelt's declaration of neutrality. A small minority of Americans believed in

A German panzer (tank) rolls through a Polish town in 1939. The German invasion of Poland marked the start of six years of world war. *(Library of Congress)*

Soviet-style communism, and an even tinier minority supported the Nazis. Most Americans sympathized with Britain and France in their fight against Nazi Germany, but that did not mean they wanted the United States to get involved in the war. Americans were more concerned about problems at home, especially the lingering depression. There was also a general feeling that this was Europe's war and that the United States should stay out of it. This attitude was known as isolationism.

The nation had a long tradition of staying out of foreign wars, but the isolationism of 1939–1941 also had its roots in the U.S. experience in World War I. When that conflict began in 1914, the United States had also tried to remain neutral. After Germany launched submarine attacks on U.S. ships, the United States entered the war in 1917, to join the Allies (Britain and France) against Germany. Some 2 million U.S. troops went to Europe; about 100,000 were killed before the war ended in an Allied victory in November 1918.

Americans in World War I believed they were fighting to make the world "safe for democracy," in President

German foreign minister Joachim von Ribbentrop and Soviet foreign minister Viacheslav Molotov sign the Nazi-Soviet Non-Aggression Pact in Moscow while Stalin (standing in light-colored jacket) looks on. *(Library of Congress)*

Regular passenger flights across the Atlantic began on June 28, 1939, when the Pan-American Airways *Dixie Clipper* lifted off from Long Island, New York, bound for Lisbon, Portugal.

Woodrow Wilson's words. Twenty years later, the same countries were now at war again. Many Americans now believed that the U.S. entry into World War I was a mistake—one that should not be repeated.

In addition, congressional investigations in the 1930s claimed to find evidence that the United States had gone to war in 1917, not to make the world safe for democracy, but to boost the profits of arms manufacturers and to make sure that Britain paid back the money it had borrowed from U.S. banks. Whether or not these claims are true is still argued, but it added to the belief that the United States should stay out of foreign wars. In an effort to keep the country from being drawn in to such conflicts, Congress passed a series of laws that made it illegal for U.S. companies to sell arms or loan money to countries at war.

As the decade of the 1940s began, Americans watched events in Europe unfold with anxiety, but with the hope that their sons, brothers, and husbands would not have to face combat. Events would soon show that the world was now too dangerous a place for the United States to remain in isolation.

CHAPTER 2

WAR BRINGS CHANGE, 1940–1941

NINETEEN FORTY WAS A PRESIDENTIAL election year. At its July convention in Chicago, the Democratic Party nominated President Franklin Delano Roosevelt as its candidate for a third term in the White House. Roosevelt's decision to run again surprised many. If elected, he would become the first president to spend more than two terms in office. At the time, the Constitution did not forbid a president from serving more than two terms, but there was a tradition

In December 1940, this Woonsocket, Rhode Island, gas station was open for business, selling evergreen trees for holiday decoration. The last prewar Christmas was shadowed by news of war, however. *(Library of Congress)*

Wendell Willkie was the Republican candidate in the presidential election of 1940. *(Private Collection)*

of not seeking a third term that went all the way back to George Washington. Roosevelt had told some friends and advisers that he did not want to run again. In the end, however, Democratic leaders persuaded the president that the country needed his continued leadership in such dangerous times. Roosevelt announced that he would run again to prevent the spread of war to U.S. shores.

Meeting in Philadelphia, the Republican Party chose Wendell Willkie as its candidate. The Indiana-born Willkie was a wealthy lawyer with little political experience, but in the 1930s he had won national attention by opposing some of Roosevelt's New Deal programs in court cases.

Unlike many Republican leaders, Willkie was not an isolationist. Like his Democratic opponent, Willkie believed in helping Britain combat Germany as much as possible while staying out of the war. For most voters, the big issue of the campaign was not the war but Roosevelt's break with tradition in running for a third term.

THE DESTROYERS FOR BASES DEAL

While the U.S. presidential campaign was underway, the situation in Europe went from bad to worse. In the spring of 1940, German forces overran and occupied Denmark, Norway, the Netherlands, and Belgium, and invaded France. In late June, France surrendered, leaving Britain alone in the fight against Nazi Germany.

The German military planned to invade Britain next, but they needed to destroy Britain's air defenses first. Throughout the summer of 1940, British and German fighter planes skirmished daily in the skies over southern England, in what came to be known as the Battle of Britain. High losses of planes and pilots eventually forced Germany to end the campaign and postpone the invasion.

Britain had escaped invasion but faced defeat by starvation in another battle—the Battle of the Atlantic.

"A simple barefoot Wall Street lawyer."

—Secretary of the Interior Harold Ickes's description of Wendell Willkie

As a small island nation, Britain depended on shipments of food, fuel, and other supplies to keep fighting and to feed its people. Ships carrying these supplies, however, had to cross thousands of miles of ocean where German U-boats (submarines) lurked. Ships bound for Britain sailed in convoys for safety, but so-called wolf packs of submarines still sent many of them to the bottom of the Atlantic.

With Britain's Royal Navy stretched to the limit, British prime minister Winston Churchill appealed to President Roosevelt for help. Churchill asked the president to transfer destroyers from U.S. Navy to the Royal Navy.

Roosevelt wanted to help, but he knew that such a move would not be acceptable to many Americans unless the United States received something in return. So Britain and the United States made a deal. The United States would send 50 destroyers (mostly them old vessels from World War I) to Britain. In return, the U.S. military received permission to build military bases in British territory in the Caribbean region and off the Atlantic coast of Canada. The president announced the Destroyers for Bases deal in early September 1940. It was the Roosevelt administration's boldest move thus far in its support of Britain. To isolationists, it was a big step closer to U.S. involvement in the war in Europe.

German dictator Adolf Hitler and his chief deputy, Herman Goering, prepare to receive France's surrender on June 22, 1940. *(Library of Congress)*

A German U-boat (submarine) is launched. *(Library of Congress)*

Workers labor on a ship under construction at the Bath Iron Works in Maine in late 1940, when the U.S. began to rearm to meet the threat from Germany. *(Library of Congress)*

THE SELECTIVE SERVICE ACT

Even if Americans opposed getting into the war, many citizens now believed that the United States had to strengthen its own defenses to face any threat from overseas. Even before the fall of France, Congress had voted an increase of more than a billion dollars in military spending. In July 1940, Congress also approved funds for the construction of new warships and fighter planes.

The U.S. Army, however, was unprepared for any major conflict in times of peace the United States traditionally maintained only a small army, whose ranks were filled by volunteers. Budget cuts in the depression years had reduced the size of the army even further. In 1940, the U.S. Army numbered only about 100,000 soldiers. The army was weak not only in numbers, but also in equipment. Many of its weapons were old and outdated.

The only way to increase the size of the army in a short time was to reintroduce conscription, or the draft, in which young men had to register with the government. If called up, they had to serve in the military for a period of time whether they wanted to or not.

In June, the bill for the Selective Service Act was introduced in Congress. The law would require U.S. men between the ages of 21 and 35 to register for the draft. If

BIRTH OF THE JEEP

In 1940, the U.S. Army asked U.S. carmakers to develop a scout car that would be light and fast but rugged enough to carry several soldiers or a 500-pound load across rough terrain. Three companies—Ford, Bantam, and Willy's Overland—each came up with separate but similar designs. The army eventually settled on a model that combined parts of all three designs. This vehicle became the famous jeep, and Willys and Ford would build more than 350,000 of the tough little cars over the next five years.

Jeeps were among the first military vehicles sent to Britain as part of Lend-Lease. After the United States entered the war, they served everywhere that U.S. forces went, from the snows of Alaska to the jungles of the South Pacific, and they were used for everything from carrying wounded to aid stations to serving as mobile chapels for religious services.

No one knows exactly how the jeep got its name. It may have come from the initials GP, for general purpose car, or from the character Eugene the Jeep in the Popeye comic strip. Jeeps remained in service with the U.S. military for an amazing 40 years, until they were replaced by the High Mobility Multipurpose Wheeled Vehicle (the Humvee) in the early 1980s.

War correspondent Ernie Pyle wrote, "I don't think we could continue the war without the jeep. It does everything. It goes everywhere. It's as faithful as a dog, strong as a mule, and as agile as a goat." *(Franklin D. Roosevelt Presidential Library and Museum)*

Among the first draftees selected by lottery was radio broadcaster Stephen McCormick, shown here pointing to his draft number. *(Library of Congress)*

One of the bestselling books of 1942 was Marion Hargrove's *See Here, Private Hargrove*— the author's humorous but realistic account of coping with army life as a draftee in the months before Pearl Harbor.

called up for military service, draftees would be required to serve for one year, but they could not be sent overseas.

There had never been a peacetime draft in the nation's history, and the fiercest isolationists attacked the bill, calling it un-American. With support from both presidential candidates Roosevelt and Wendell Willkie, the bill became law in September 1940, and soon some 16 million men were registered. The first draftees were chosen by lottery later that year.

The army scrambled to house and train the new draftees. Old bases were reopened and newer ones were built, mostly in the southern states, where the weather was warm and training could go on year-round.

The army was on its way to having the soldiers it needed, but equipping them would take time. Many draftees wore uniforms from the World War I era. At first, painted logs had to stand in for artillery pieces, and ordinary cars with the word *tank* painted on their sides took the place of real tanks in training exercises.

THE AMERICA FIRST COMMITTEE

The passage of the Selective Service Act and the announcement of the Destroyers for Bases deal led to fierce protests from isolationists. There were already hundreds of citizens' groups opposed to any involvement in the war, and in September 1940, several isolationist leaders formed the America First Committee. The committee's founders included well-known politicians, writers, and entertainers.

At the committee's first big rally, in Chicago in September, thousands of people cheered speakers who accused President Roosevelt of being a warmonger. Within a year, the committee had a membership of about 800,000 people.

Other Americans, however, were changing their minds about aiding Britain in the fall of 1940. After Hitler decided not to invade Britain, Germany now tried to bomb Britain into surrender. Starting in September, fleets of German bombers began raiding London and other British cities. The bombing campaign lasted years and killed about 60,000 British civilians.

"I have said this before, but I shall say it again and again: Your boys are not going to be sent into any foreign wars."

—President Roosevelt in a campaign speech in Boston, October 30, 1940

Four of the leaders of the America First Committee appear together. From left to right are Montana senator Burton Wheeler, pilot Charles Lindbergh, writer Kathleen Norris, and socialist leader Norman Thomas. *(Library of Congress)*

On November 1, the Mount Rushmore Memorial officially opened. The massive monument, designed by sculptor John Borglum, featured the faces of four U.S. presidents— Washington, Jefferson, Lincoln, and Theodore Roosevelt—carved into the rock of South Dakota's Black Hills.

Thanks to radio, people could now listen to news when it happened, and U.S. reporters, such as Edward R. Murrow, made dramatic live broadcasts from London. Americans sitting in their living rooms heard the sounds of bombs exploding and the screech of sirens. Despite the bombing of its cities and the battlefield defeats in the Mediterranean region and North Africa, Britain hung on.

Britain's brave stand against Germany and the stirring speeches of Winston Churchill convinced many Americans of the need to aid Britain and any other nation willing to fight to Germany and its allies, Italy and Japan. Groups such as the Committee to Defend America by Aiding the Allies gained new members. But polls continued to show that only a minority of Americans, dubbed Interventionists, favored actually getting into the war.

THE ELECTION AND LEND-LEASE

On November 5, 1940, Americans went to the polls and reelected Franklin Roosevelt as president. The popular vote was 22 million for Willkie, 25 million for Roosevelt. It was not a landslide victory for Roosevelt, but it showed that the majority of Americans backed the president and his policies. Roosevelt's party, the Democrats, held their majority in the House of Representatives. With his political position secure, the president soon announced a proposal to continue aid to Britain.

According to the so-called cash-and-carry policy, Britain had to pay for military supplies from the United States. By this time, however, the British government was nearly broke. It no longer had the money to pay for U.S. food, fuel, and weapons. Speaking to reporters in mid-December, Roosevelt proposed changing the law to allow the United States to send goods to Britain without immediate payment. Britain would receive the goods

THE LONE EAGLE FALLS

The most well known leader of the America First Committee was pilot Charles Lindbergh, who had won worldwide fame in 1927 by making the first flight across the Atlantic from New York to Paris. Speaking at a rally in Des Moines, Iowa, Lindbergh said that he believed (like the British government and the Roosevelt administration), that Jewish Americans were responsible for "pressing this country toward war." The speech offended many Americans, as did the fact that Lindbergh had accepted medals from the German air force after Hitler came to power in the 1930s. President Roosevelt was so furious with Lindbergh that when war came and Lindbergh volunteered for military service, Roosevelt made sure that Lindbergh was turned away. Lindbergh did manage to fly in the Pacific as a civilian consultant later during the war, which did not stop him from (unofficially) shooting down at least one Japanese plane.

On October 27, 1940, the New York World's Fair closed its doors. Some 25 million people had visited the fair since its opening on April 30, 1939.

Charles Lindbergh (right) and his wife, Anne, are shown here with Nazi leader Herman Goering, head of the Luftwaffe, in 1938. *(Library of Congress)*

Londoners pick through the wreckage of their homes, destroyed by German bombs during the Blitz that lasted from late 1940 to May 1941. *(Library of Congress)*

Edward R. Murrow's broadcasts from England brought the reality of war home to Americans. *(Library of Congress)*

when needed and pay the government back after the war, either in money or goods and services.

"Suppose my neighbor's home catches fire," Roosevelt explained. "If he can take my garden hose and connect it up with his hydrant, I may help him to put out his fire . . . I do not say to him before that operation, 'Neighbor, my garden hose cost me $15; you have to pay me $15 for it'. . . I don't want $15—I want my garden hose back after the fire."

The system Roosevelt proposed, which would come to be called Lend-Lease, was not quite that simple. There was no guarantee Britain would survive the war against Germany. Even if it did, most of the material the United States shipped to Britain would probably be damaged or destroyed by the time the war was over—unlike the garden hose in Roosevelt's example.

The president took the case for Lend-Lease to Americans in a radio speech on December 29, 1940. Although he once again said he had no intention of entering the war, Roosevelt said that the United States must become "the arsenal of democracy," sending as

RADIO DAYS

Even when all anyone seemed to care about was the progress of the Nazis across Europe, Americans gathered around the radio for more than news. Popular comedies included Fanny Brice's *Baby Snooks* and *The Bickersons,* starring Don Ameche and Frances Langford. Both programs were written by Philip Rapp, who became a successful screenwriter after the war.

Fanny Brice was a well known vaudeville entertainer of the 1920s and 1930s, whose life became the subject of the Broadway musical and movie *Funny Girl.* Her Baby Snooks character, created in 1937, became immensely popular as the main character of a radio show of the same name. Brice voiced the bratty, precocious little girl who made insightful comments about the adult world throughout the 1940s, until her death in 1951.

The Bickersons was a fast-paced, witty show featuring a married couple, John and Blanche, who fought constantly. Their relentless insults flew back and forth in sharp exchanges that nonetheless made listeners laugh. Don Ameche went on to a long career in movies that lasted until the 1980s; Frances Langford appeared in *Yankee Doodle Dandy* (1942) and other films throughout the war and retired in the 1960s.

much help as possible to any nation resisting the aggression of Nazi Germany and its allies.

Throughout the first months of 1941, Americans debated Lend-Lease in the newspapers, on the streets, and in Congress. Isolationists bitterly opposed the Lend-Lease Act, on the grounds that it would lead the United States into war. Senator Burton Wheeler of Montana said that Lend-Lease would "plow under every fourth American boy." Others felt that the proposed bill would give too much power to Roosevelt. The Lend-Lease act left it up to the president to decide which nations would receive aid and the amount and kind of aid they would receive.

The bill managed to pass both houses of Congress, and President Roosevelt signed it into law on March 12, 1941. By the end of the year, the United States had shipped more than a thousand tanks to Britain, along with a million pounds of food; and huge quantities of weapons, ammunition, and other supplies.

U.S. mills, factories, and farms were able to do all this while at the same time producing the goods for the nation's own fast-growing army, air force, and navy. To speed up the process, Congress provided money to U.S. companies to help finance the cost of converting factories from the production of civilian goods to military

"What I am trying to do . . . is to get rid of the silly, foolish old dollar sign."

—President Roosevelt in another explanation of his idea for Lend-Lease

In addition to explosive bombs, the German Luftwaffe (Air Force) used incendiary bombs to start fires in its raids on London. Here, firefighters hose down a burned-out building. *(Library of Congress)*

gear. The nation's automakers, for example, reduced their production of cars by one-fifth so that more tanks and other military vehicles could be produced.

Across the nation, factories that had been shuttered and silent since the early 1930s roared back to life as orders for wartime goods poured in. The unemployment rate, which had been stuck at more than 10 percent for years, dropped as companies employed millions.

ACTION IN THE NORTH ATLANTIC

Producing goods for Britain's war effort was one thing; shipping those goods to Britain was another. German U-boats continued to sink many ships, while Britain-bound convoys were also vulnerable to attack from German submarines and planes.

After the passage of the Lend-Lease Act, President Roosevelt took steps to protect the sea lanes (heavily traveled shipping routes) from the United States to Britain. In July, U.S. troops landed on the island of Iceland to keep German forces from using it as a base. (Denmark, which governed Iceland at this time, had earlier been conquered

by Germany in April.) U.S. forces also went ashore on Greenland in North America, another Danish territory.

The president authorized a safety zone that extended from the East Coast of the United States to Iceland, most of the way across the Atlantic. Within that zone, U.S. warships helped the British and Canadian navies protect cargo ships. In addition, U.S. naval commanders were ordered to help the Royal Navy locate German ships and aircraft. In May 1941, for example, the British navy sank the mighty German battleship *Bismarck;* the *Bismarck* was caught after being sighted by a U.S.-made Royal Navy patrol plane whose crew included a U.S. pilot.

With the United States now openly helping Britain in the Battle of the Atlantic, it was not long before U.S. and German vessels clashed. Although at first the

Officers aboard a U.S. Navy destroyer keep a sharp lookout for German submarines while guarding a convoy of supply ships during the Battle of the Atlantic. *(Library of Congress)*

"This . . . is London."

—CBS reporter
Edward R. Murrow,
introducing one of his
live radio broadcasts from
the bomb-ravaged city

MURROW'S BOYS

Edward R. Murrow was the lead correspondent for CBS Radio in London. His tag line at the start of every broadcast became one of the most well known phrases in popular culture at the time. But Murrow was not the only CBS correspondent.

Eric Sevareid, Howard K. Smith, Charles Collingwood, Richard C. Gottelet, Bill Downs, and Winston Burdette also reported regularly for CBS. Their voices became familiar; before the days of television, Americans had to rely on the CBS correspondents' verbal descriptions to imagine what was happening. Many of them went on to distinguished careers as television newscasters in the 1950s and 1960s.

One CBS broadcaster, William Shirer, reported from Berlin, Germany, before the war. He later went on to write two of the most famous books about Germany in that era, *Berlin Diary* and *The Rise and Fall of the Third Reich*.

Edward R. Murrow, stationed in London, and William L. Shirer, in Berlin, were both CBS broadcasters during World War II who went on to illustrious careers. *(Library of Congress)*

German navy was ordered not to attack U.S. cargo ships, a German U-boat sank the U.S. freighter *Robin Moore* in late May 1941, leading an angry Roosevelt to declare "an unlimited state of national emergency."

In August, President Roosevelt and Prime Minister Churchill met aboard a warship off the coast of

CITIZEN KANE

One of the notable movies of 1941 was *Citizen Kane,* written and directed by Orson Welles, who also acted the title role. Although he was only 26 years old, Welles was already famous, because of his brilliant radio dramas. (One of them, based on the science-fiction story The *War of the Worlds,* was so realistic that it caused a nationwide panic in 1938 after some listeners became convinced that aliens from space had landed in New Jersey.) *Kane* is the story of a newspaper publisher who achieves fame and wealth but winds up lonely and heartbroken. Welles based the movie on a real-life person, the powerful publisher William Randolph Hearst. Hearst was not happy at seeing his life fictionalized on the big screen. He used his considerable power to keep as many theaters as he could from showing the movie. Many movie critics now consider *Citizen Kane* one of the best, and perhaps *the* best, U.S. film of all time.

Orson Welles appeared in the role of Charles Foster Kane in *Citizen Kane. (Private Collection)*

Newfoundland in Canada. The two leaders drew up a document, the Atlantic Charter, which outlined their goals for the postwar world, including free trade and closer cooperation among nations in the interests of peace. It also pledged U.S. support for the "final destruction of Nazi tyranny." The Atlantic Charter was not a military or political alliance between the United States and Britain, exactly, but it pledged the two nations to achieve a common end.

By this time, Britain was no longer fighting alone. In June 1941, Hitler had broken his Non-Aggression Pact with Stalin by launching a massive invasion of the Soviet Union. Although many Americans felt that Stalin was just as evil a dictator as Hitler, the Soviet Union began to receive Lend-Lease shipments.

In the fall, clashes between U.S. and German ships increased. In October, 11 sailors died when a U-boat torpedoed the U.S. destroyer USS *Kearny,* which was protecting a convoy sailing south of Iceland. Two weeks later another German torpedo sunk the destroyer USS *Reuben James,* causing the loss of 115 men. The president now gave the U.S. Navy orders to attack any

William Randolph Hearst did everything he could to stop Orson Welles from making *Citizen Kane* and to stop people from seeing it after it was released. *(Library of Congress)*

Women soldiers of the British Army carry a few of the 500,00 U.S.-made rifles shipped to Britain under Lend-Lease. *(Library of Congress)*

German planes or vessels in the safety zone. As the last weeks of 1941 began, the United States was edging closer to war with Germany. The event that finally brought the nation into the war fully, however, took place not in the chilly waters of the North Atlantic, but in the warm blue seas around the Pacific islands of Hawaii, which was then a U.S. territory.

THE TRIPARTITE PACT

Throughout 1940 and 1941, Americans from the president on down were most concerned with the war in Europe, but on the other side of the world, Japan continued its war against China. In September 1940, Japan joined Germany and Italy in an agreement called the Tripartite (three-power) Pact. The three nations, also know as the Axis, promised to support each other if one was attacked by the United States or another nation. The agreement also recognized Japan's wish to be the dominant power in Asia. The Rome-Berlin Axis now extended to include Tokyo, the capital of Japan. The conflict that had begun in Poland in 1939 was now truly a world war.

Japan's ongoing war with China and its move into Indochina (southeast Asia) angered many Americans, including President Roosevelt. The United States began strengthening the defenses of its territories and possessions in the Pacific, including the Philippine Islands. The United States also sent ships and planes to Pearl Harbor, the chief U.S. military base in the Pacific, located on the Hawaiian island of Oahu.

As much as most Americans opposed Japan's moves in Asia, they did not want to go to war with Japan in 1940–41, just as they did not want to enter the war in Europe. But the U.S. government did have a way to put pressure on Japan short of military action.

Like Britain, Japan was a small island nation with few natural resources. It needed to import almost all of the fuel and metal its army and navy needed to continue the war in China and to carry out its plans for conquest in the rest of Asia and the Pacific. Japan imported much of its fuel and steel in the form of oil and scrap metal from the United States. In summer 1941, President Roosevelt ordered a halt to exports of these materials to Japan. That nation, however, refused to leave Indochina or China.

British soldiers stack cases of U.S.-made explosives in an underground tunnel. *(Library of Congress)*

A Sherman tank is hoisted aboard a freighter for shipment to Britain. By late 1941 the British were using Shermans in their campaign in Egypt and Libya. *(Library of Congress)*

In the fall, Japanese and U.S. diplomats tried to ease the tensions between the two nations, but they made no progress. In early December 1941, President Roosevelt decided to send a personal letter to the emperor of Japan, appealing for peace. By the time the letter was ready, however, war was less than a day away.

JAPAN'S GAMBLE

The real power in Japan was held not by the emperor but by the military officers who controlled the government. These admirals and generals believed that quick military action was the only way for Japan to secure the resources it needed. In the end, the Japanese military leadership decided on what they called the Southern Strategy of conquest in the Pacific.

Japan's leading admiral, Yamamoto Isoroku, was in charge of planning these operations. Many Japanese officers believed that the United States was a big but weak nation whose people had no stomach for war and who would back off if challenged by Japan. Yamamoto was not one of them. He had lived in the United States and respected the power of U.S. industry and the willpower of Americans when their anger was aroused. Yamamoto believed that the only way for Japan to conquer Asia was to deliver a surprise knockout blow to destroy the U.S. fleet. This plan would give Japan time to complete its Asian conquest before the United States could recover and strike back.

The centerpiece of Yamamoto's plan was an air raid on the U.S. base at Pearl Harbor. It was a daring and complicated operation. Three Japanese aircraft carriers would have to cross thousands of miles of ocean without being detected in order to achieve the surprise attack. In late November 1941, the Pearl Harbor task force sailed from Japan.

By this time, U.S. Navy codebreakers had cracked many of the codes used by Japan's military and

BLACKOUTS

Although no air raids occurred on the U.S. mainland, the Office of Civilian Defense (OCD), created in May 1941, tried to prepare Americans for such an event. New York mayor Fiorello La Guardia, with First Lady Eleanor Roosevelt as his official assistant, was in charge of the OCD and quickly instituted a system of air raid wardens and sirens.

U.S. military officials soon decreed that nighttime blackouts were necessary. They feared that the bright lights of cities would lead enemy bombers to important targets such as Detroit or San Francisco. Outdoor lights, such as streetlights, were darkened during

Fiorello La Guardia, popular mayor of New York City, was named head of the Office of Civilian Defense. *(Library of Congress)*

blackouts. Indoor lights were only permitted in rooms hung with blackout curtains or shades.

Americans purchased thousands of yards of heavy black cloth to cover their windows. Often families would gather together in the blackout-curtained rooms to read or play games together. Still, the mood was not too bleak. *House and Garden* magazine reminded homemakers that "Bedrooms need not go into mourning," and suggested that housewives should "Make a blackout shade by seaming together two pieces of fabric, one black and one to match your curtain."

JOLTIN' JOE'S STREAK

In the summer of 1941, baseball fans watched breathlessly as Joe DiMaggio of the New York Yankees went on one of sports history's greatest winning streaks. From May 15 to July 17, the Yankee Clipper hit safely in 56 games in a row, until the Cleveland Indians managed to keep him off base in front of a crowd of more than 67,000. (The Yankees managed to win the game 4-3 anyway.) DiMaggio's streak shattered the previous record for hitting safely by 15 games, and his record still stands untouched as of 2005.

Joe Dimaggio helped the Yankees win ten pennants and nine World Series from 1936 to 1951. He served in the U.S. Army from 1943 through 1945. *(National Baseball Hall of Fame Library and Museum)*

diplomatic services to communicate in secret. Recent messages indicated that an attack was about to occur somewhere in the Pacific, but the codes were not completely broken, so the United States did not know the target. Few expected an attack on Pearl Harbor, even though the U.S. ambassador to Japan, Joseph Grew, had reported "a lot of talk" in Tokyo about an upcoming attack on Hawaii.

Nevertheless, a warning message was sent from Washington, D.C., to the army and navy commanders in Hawaii. Unfortunately, like the president's letter to the emperor, the warning came too late. By the time the message was delivered, bombs were already falling on Pearl Harbor.

DAY OF INFAMY

At around 7:30 A.M. on the sunny Sunday morning of December 7, 1941, about 150 Japanese warplanes took off from their aircraft carriers and flew low over Oahu. An army radar station detected the attacking planes, but operators thought they were U.S. planes traveling with a flight of U.S. Army Air Force bombers being flown to Hawaii from California that morning.

At just before 8:00 A.M., the Japanese planes began raining bombs and torpedoes on Pearl Harbor's Battleship Row, where the big warships of the U.S. Pacific Fleet lay at anchor, many of their crews still asleep in their bunks.

Explosions rocked ship after ship. Just a few minutes after the first wave of Japanese planes departed, a second wave of some 150 aircraft arrived to continue their deadly work. Other Japanese planes shot up nearby Wheeler and Hickam airfields, where Army Air Force planes were parked in neat rows on the runways.

The raid lasted about two hours and left Pearl Harbor full of smoking wreckage and floating bodies. About 2,300 sailors, marines, and soldiers were killed (more than a thousand alone on the battleship USS *Arizona*, which exploded after a direct hit) as well as approximately 70 civilians. More than 1,000 others were wounded. Nineteen U.S. ships, including eight battleships, were sunk or heavily damaged, along with more than 150 planes. The Japanese lost only 29 planes to U.S. anti-aircraft fire or to the machine guns of the few U.S. fighters that managed to get into the air.

Because of the time difference between Hawaii and the eastern United States, the first reports of the attack did not reach most Americans until early Sunday afternoon. Many people heard the news when announcers interrupted football games or concerts on the radio.

Every American who was more than a few years old on that day would always remember where they were and what they were doing when they heard the

Many Americans first heard of the attack on Pearl Harbor when news bulletins interrupted the popular Sunday afternoon radio broadcast of the NBC Symphony Orchestra. The orchestra's conductor, Arturo Toscanini, was a refugee from Fascist Italy.

A cartoon published in *Time* magazine two weeks after Pearl Harbor shows Japanese Admiral Isoroku Yamamato, mastermind of the attack. *(Library of Congress)*

The battleship *Arizona* sinks in flames after taking a direct hit from a Japanese bomb. Of the 2,400 Americans killed at Pearl Harbor, more than half died aboard the *Arizona*. *(Franklin D. Roosevelt Presidential Library and Museum)*

Women firefighters, most of them Asian Americans, helped fight the blazes set by Japanese bombs at Pearl Harbor— thus becoming the first American women to rush to the country's defense during World War II.

news of the attack. Like November 22, 1963 (the day President John F. Kennedy was assassinated), and September 11, 2001 (when terrorists destroyed New York's World Trade Center), December 7, 1941, was a date that would be burned into the minds of a generation of Americans.

As terrible as the attack was, it was not the knockout blow that Admiral Yamamoto wanted. For one thing, the U.S. Pacific Fleet's aircraft carriers were at sea on the morning of December 7 and so they escaped destruction or damage. The coming war in the Pacific would prove that U.S. aircraft carriers, not big battleships like the ones sunk at Pearl Harbor, were the key to victory at sea.

In addition, the Japanese concentrated on destroying ships and planes rather than the fuel tanks and repair shops around Pearl Harbor. In the months ahead, these facilities would keep the surviving U.S. warships at sea and repair many of those damaged and sunk in the attack. The Japanese also ignored Pearl Harbor's submarine base. In a few years, submarines would play an important role in winning the war in the Pacific by sinking practically all of the cargo ships on which Japan's war effort depended.

DORIE MILLER

In the segregated U.S. Navy of 1941, most African-American sailors were restricted to such jobs as working in ships' messes (dining areas) and galleys (kitchens) and were rarely allowed to serve in gun crews or perform other combat roles. During the attack on Pearl Harbor, however, an African-American cook aboard the battleship USS *West Virginia,* Doris "Dorie" Miller, proved that a sailor's race had nothing to do with his courage or coolness under fire. When the raid began, Miller carried several wounded sailors to safety. He then fired a machine gun at the attacking Japanese aircraft until he ran out of ammunition. For his bravery, Miller became the first African American to receive the Navy Cross, one of the nation's highest decorations. Miller continued to serve with distinction until he went down with his ship, the air- craft carrier *Liscome Bay,* after a Japanese submarine torpedoed it in November 1943.

"above and beyond the call of duty"

DORIE MILLER
Received the Navy Cross at Pearl Harbor, May 27, 1942

The U.S. Office of War Information published this poster to celebrate Dorie Miller's courage at Pearl Harbor. It appeared in 1943, shortly after Miller was killed in action. *(Library of Congress)*

All this, however, was in the future on the afternoon of December 7. All that Americans knew then was that a territory of their country had been attacked without warning, by the forces of a nation with which the United States was at peace. (Japanese diplomats had prepared to announce that Japan was breaking off relations with the United States on the morning of December 7, but they, too, had communication problems. The announcement arrived just as word of the attack reached U.S. leaders.)

The following morning President Roosevelt addressed both houses of Congress. Gripping the sides of the podium, his face full of anger but his voice strong

With sadness and grim determination showing in his face, President Roosevelt signs Congress's Declaration of War against Japan on December 8, 1941. *(Library of Congress)*

and clear, he began, "Yesterday, December 7, 1941—a date which will live in infamy—the United States of America was suddenly and deliberately attacked by naval and air forces of the Empire of Japan."

At the end of his speech, he called on Congress to declare war against Japan, which it did within a few minutes of convening. The only no vote came from Representative Jeanette Rankin of Montana, a pacifist who had also voted against U.S. entry into World War I 24 years earlier.

The attack united Americans in shock and anger. The debate between isolationists and interventionists ended immediately. The America First Committee voted itself out of existence the following morning. Instead of collapsing in shock, as some Japanese leaders thought would happen, Americans now thirsted for revenge against Japan.

On December 11, Germany and Italy kept to the terms of the Tripartite Pact with Japan and declared war on the United States. This development surprised some observers because Hitler was not known for keeping agreements, as the German invasion of the Soviet Union had proved. Congress quickly voted to recognize that "a state of war" existed between the United States and Germany and Italy as well as Japan. After more than two years of trying to stay out of the fight, the United States was now at war around the world.

Winston Churchill later wrote that after President Roosevelt phoned to tell him of the attack on Pearl Harbor he went to bed and slept soundly for the first time in months, because he knew that with the United States in the war, the democracies would eventually defeat the forces of tyranny. There would be many dark days, however, before that victory was won.

CHAPTER 3

THE WAR AT HOME AND AT SEA, 1942–1943

"JAPANESE BOMBS," WROTE *TIME* MAG-azine a week after the attack on Pearl Harbor, "had finally brought national unity." For one group of Americans, however, fear and anger over Pearl Harbor quickly led to the loss of their homes, property, and rights. This group included Americans of Japanese birth (who called themselves *Issei*) and children of Japanese-born parents (*Nissci*), who were eventually sent to internment camps such as Manzanar.

About 127,000 Japanese Americans lived in the continental United States in 1941, mostly in California. About two-thirds of them were U.S. citizens. Another 158,000 lived in the territory of Hawaii.

Japanese-American Tom Kobayashi gazes at the distant hills at the Manzanar Relocation Camp, in the desert about 200 miles northeast of Los Angeles. *(Library of Congress)*

THE OTHER "ENEMIES"

There were about 127,000 people of Japanese birth or ancestry living in the United States in December 1941. About 500,000 other enemy aliens (Americans of German, Italian, Hungarian, or Romanian birth who were not U.S. citizens) were also living in the United States. However, these people did not suffer the same fate as the Japanese Americans. About 10,000 German Americans, who were suspected of disloyalty, were interned during the war, as well as with several hundred Italian Americans. Several thousand other Italian Americans who lived in coastal areas were forbidden to move from their homes, although these restrictions were lifted after the Allied invasion of Italy in 1943.

The differing treatment of Japanese Americans and German and Italian Americans reflected the racial attitudes held by many Americans in the 1940s. Most Americans at this time were of European ancestry. While they hated nazism and fascism, they did not feel the same bitterness toward the nation's European enemies as they did toward the Japanese. Most Americans knew little of Japanese history and culture, and after Pearl Harbor many Americans viewed the Japanese as inhuman monsters. It was this hatred for anything to do with Japan, combined with the anger over Pearl Harbor, that created the climate of fear that led to Executive Order 9066.

Although nearly 158,000 Japanese Americans lived in the territory of Hawaii, there was no internment on the islands, except for a few Japanese Americans suspected of spying for Japan. The authorities considered interning the Japanese Americans of Hawaii but decided there were just too many to make such a program practical.

"Greetings. Having submitted yourself to a local board composed of your neighbors for the purposes of determining your availability for training or service in the land or naval forces of the United States, you are hereby notified that you are now selected..."

—Draft notice, 1942

In the fearful days after Pearl Harbor, many Americans believed the Japanese were about to invade Hawaii or even the West Coast. Rumors flew that Japanese Americans were spying for Japan. In fact, no Japanese American on the West Coast was ever found guilty of a disloyal act during the war. That did not keep people from demanding that the government move their Japanese-American neighbors away from the coast. As public pressure mounted, California attorney general Earl Warren asked President Roosevelt to order the relocation of Japanese Americans.

On February 19, 1942, President Roosevelt, vowing to maintain national security, signed Executive Order 9066. It gave the federal government the power to define "military areas...from which any or all persons may be excluded as deemed necessary or desirable." The order did not mention Japanese Americans by name, but they were the "any and all persons."

Between March and August 1942, 112,000 Japanese Americans in California, Oregon, Washington, and Arizona were ordered to report to relocation centers. Most of those to be relocated had to abandon their homes, businesses, and farms, or sell them for little money. Those who were U.S. citizens were stripped of the right to vote.

From the relocation centers, the detained Japanese Americans were taken to inland internment camps far from their homes. Most of the camps were in bleak, remote places, such as Tule Lake and Manzanar in northern California. The camps were cramped and uncomfortable places, where families were forced to live in small spaces and had to make do with crude facilities for cooking and bathing. The barbed wire and guard towers were especially humiliating to the internees, most of whom considered themselves loyal U.S. citizens.

The crude barracks at Manzanar housed almost 10,000 Japanese Americans who had been taken from their California homes.
(Library of Congress)

As the most glamorous of the services, the USAAF was a popular choice for volunteers, although relatively few met the tough standards for pilot training. *(Library of Congress)*

Because of anger over Pearl Harbor, few Japanese Americans dared to speak out against this huge violation of their rights as U.S. citizens. In December 1944, however, the issue reached the U.S. Supreme Court when Fred Korematsu, a Nissei, challenged the relocation order. The Court ruled that Executive Order 9066 was justified by "military necessity."

By that time fears of a Japanese invasion had faded. The internees began to be released. Not until 1968 did they receive compensation for the property they had lost. In 1990, the federal government apologized to the surviving internees.

THE RUSH TO SERVE

In the weeks after the attack on Pearl Harbor, hundreds of thousands of Americans crowded into recruiting centers to enlist in the U.S. Army, Navy, and Marine Corps. Many were sent home and told to come back later. Even with the military expansion of 1940–41, there were not enough training camps, uniforms, and weapons to go around.

There would be plenty of opportunity to serve. More than 16 million Americans (including about 350,000 women) would wear their country's uniform between 1941 and the war's end in August 1945. This was more than 12 percent of the total population.

Not everyone could serve. Over the course of the war, the military turned down about one in three volunteers and draftees because of physical or mental problems. Men with special skills needed in the civilian workforce also were not subject to the draft. But most men between the ages of 18 and 36 served in the military between 1941 and 1945.

Some men simply waited for their draft notice, the letter ordering them to report for duty. In late December 1941, Congress revised the Selective Service Act, making all men between the ages of 18 and 44 eligible to be

GO FOR BROKE

Despite the internment, more than 10,000 Japanese Americans volunteered for military service during the war, many of them straight out of the internment camps. Several all-Nisei units were formed, the most famous of which was the U.S. Army's 442nd Regimental Combat Team, whose motto was "Go for broke!" The 442nd served with great distinction in fierce fighting in Italy from 1943 to 1945. The unit had the highest casualty rate of any army unit (about 600 killed and 10,000 wounded), and its men earned more medals and decorations than any other unit as well. Among the 442nd's officers was a young Hawaiian Nisei named Daniel Inouye, who lost an arm in combat. Inouye went on to become the first Japanese American elected to the U.S. Senate.

Japanese-American men in Hawaii line up to volunteer for the unit that would become the 442nd Regimental Combat Team. *(Library of Congress)*

called up for service. Of the 16 million Americans who served, about 10 million were drafted.

Whether volunteer or draftee, the U.S. serviceman of World War II was known as a G.I. This abbreviation stood for "government issue," because all of his equipment—from his weapon to his toothbrush—was supplied by the U.S. government.

Most enlisted men (11,260,000) served in the U.S. Army, which at that time included the U.S. Air Force; 3,942,000 served in the U.S. Navy; 670,000 in the U.S. Marine Corps; and 241,000 in the U.S. Coast Guard. In addition, about 215,000 civilian sailors of the U.S. Merchant Marine crewed the ships that brought troops and supplies to the battlefronts around the world.

About three-quarters of those who served spent at least some time overseas. However, the number of soldiers, sailors, marines, and airmen who saw combat was relatively small. The U.S. military was a huge, complex organization that required many specialists—cooks, clerks, truck drivers, mechanics, and so on. At least half of all the jobs in the armed forces did not involve carrying a weapon. In any case, everyone who served received basic combat training.

A glum G.I. does K.P. duty at Fort Belvoir, Virginia, in 1942. *(Library of Congress)*

The weapon of most U.S. soldiers and marines was the semiautomatic M-1, or Garand rifle, which could fire eight times without reloading. The only semiautomatic rifle used in large numbers by any nation during World War II, the Garand gave U.S. troops a big advantage in firepower.

A new G.I.'s journey to war began with a farewell to family and friends and a journey by rail to a training camp. There the new soldier, marine, or sailor received a short haircut, a uniform that never seemed to fit, and his own bunk in a barracks that he shared with hundreds of others.

Basic training included long days of marching, hiking, and exercises and practice with rifles, grenades, and other weapons. There were also classes in military subjects, guard duty, and the dreaded K.P. (kitchen police) duty—peeling potatoes, scrubbing pots, and other chores.

Many men who had grown up during the depression found the food better and the work easier than what they were used to at home. For others, the lack of privacy, hard work, and rough living conditions made for a difficult adjustment. Learning to take orders from officers and noncommissioned officers, or sergeants, also took some getting used to for young Americans who had been raised in a society that prized individual freedom.

After basic training, men moved on to learn various specialties—tanks, radio communications, and submarines, to name a few. Those who passed the tough test for flight school began to earn their pilot's wings. College graduates and those who scored highly on intelligence tests sometimes trained to become officers.

The U.S. military of World War II was a reflection of U.S. society. Because a college education often guaranteed a spot in officer training, many (but by no means all) officers tended to come from wealthier families, because few Americans could afford the cost of college in those days. But plenty of stockbrokers' and businessmen's sons served as enlisted men alongside the sons of coal miners and farmers. Once a man or woman was in uniform, it did not matter where their ancestors came from, or whether they worshipped in a church or in a synagogue.

The military mixed up people from different parts of the country, as well as from different social classes and ethnic groups. An infantry company or ship's crew often included men from dozens of different states. A young man who had never been out of Texas might find himself becoming best friends with someone who had spent his whole life in New York City.

AFRICAN AMERICANS IN THE MILITARY

Unfortunately, the U.S. military in World War II also reflected the ugly prejudices that were part of U.S. society at this time. Prejudice and discrimination was especially intense toward African Americans.

More than 2.5 million African-American men and women either registered for the draft or volunteered for service. Once in the military, however, they faced a system of segregation similar to that found in the South. In the U.S. Army, African Americans served in segregated

Two African-American soldiers stand outside a barbershop in Columbus, Georgia. *(Library of Congress)*

In June 1942, African-American leaders met in Chicago to found the Congress of Racial Equality (CORE). Together with the older National Association for the Advancement of Colored People (NAACP), CORE became one of the nation's leading civil rights organizations.

all-black units, which were often commanded by white officers. (By the end of the war, however, the U.S. Army had about 5,000 African-American officers.)

The U.S. Army and the U.S. Army Air Force included many African-American fighting units that served bravely in combat during the war. Nevertheless, many white officers believed that African Americans were not reliable combat soldiers and that they lacked the intelligence needed for technical jobs. As a result of this attitude, many African Americans spent the war doing construction work and other backbreaking, thankless jobs behind the lines.

In the navy, African Americans had even fewer opportunities than in the army. In 1942, however, President Roosevelt ordered the navy to offer better jobs to African-American sailors. The Marine Corps refused to accept African Americans until late in the war.

In military camps in the United States, racial tensions between African-American soldiers and white soldiers and civilians sometimes exploded into violence.

The fact that most training camps were located in the South, where prejudice against African Americans was widespread, contributed to this problem.

Racial conflict took place overseas, too. For example, there was no segregation in Britain, where many U.S. troops were stationed during the buildup to the invasion of German-occupied Europe in June 1944. Some white soldiers objected to African-American soldiers relaxing in pubs or dancing with British women. There were many fights and even some deaths as white and African-American soldiers clashed. The prejudice shown by some white American soldiers puzzled and saddened many British civilians. "I like the Yanks," one was heard to say, "but I don't like these white fellows they've brought over with them."

WOMEN IN THE MILITARY

At the time of Pearl Harbor, the only women in the U.S. military were the 7,700 nurses who served in the U.S. Army and Navy Nurse corps. By the end of the war, there were more than 70,000 nurses helping the sick and wounded from Alaska to Australia. More than 200 nurses gave their lives. By late 1944, the need for nurses was so great that Secretary of War Henry Stimson asked Congress to pass a bill allowing female civilian nurses to be drafted into the military. The bill passed the House of Representatives, but the war ended before it could become law.

Many women wanted to serve their country in uniform, and not just in a nurse's uniform. The early 1940s, however, was a time when many Americans still held the view that a woman's place is in the home. Some newspapers and politicians made fun of the very idea of women in the military. Despite this attitude, Congress passed a law creating the Women's Auxiliary Army Corps (WAAC) in May 1942. About 13,000 women volunteered for the WAAC immediately. A year later, the

A 1943 poster recruits young women for the Women's Army Auxiliary Corps (WAAC). *(Library of Congress)*

Representatives of all the women's services including WAVEs and WAACs, and women's branches of the U.S. Marines, Coast Guard, and Army Air Force, show off their uniforms in this publicity photo. *(U.S. Army)*

WAAC became the Women's Army Corps (WAC) under the command of Colonel Oveta Culp Hobby.

More than 100,000 women served in the WAC during the war, about 20,000 of them overseas. The WACs served in their own units, rather than alongside male soldiers, and they were not allowed in combat. Nevertheless, WACs did many jobs that did not involve a weapon, from driving military vehicles to packing parachutes to air-traffic control.

The navy followed suit in July 1942 by establishing the Women Accepted for Volunteer Emergency Service (WAVES), in which 86,000 women served under the command of Lieutenant Commander Mildred McAfee. Later in the year the Marine Corps authorized the enlistment of women into its reserve force, and the Coast Guard set up a women's reserve, popularly known as SPARS—an acronym taken from the Coast Guard's Latin motto, *semper pavatus,* meaning "always ready." More than 1,000 female fliers served as WASPs (Women's Airforce Service Pilots), who delivered military aircraft from factories to U.S. Army Air Force bases in the United States and overseas.

FIGHTING BACK IN THE PACIFIC

Americans reading newspapers and listening to radios found mostly bad news as 1941 ended and 1942 began. By the end of December 1941, Japanese forces had captured two U.S.-held Pacific islands, Wake and Guam, and landed in the Philippines. In the Philippines, U.S. general Douglas MacArthur left the city of Manila and retreated to the Bataan Peninsula with about 75,000 U.S. and Filipino troops.

Bataan's defenders, many of them sick and all of them starving, bravely held off the invading Japanese, but there was no way to get help to the U.S. and Filipino soldiers. In March 1942, President Roosevelt ordered MacArthur to escape to Australia. The following month the surviving troops on Bataan surrendered to the Japanese. Thousands of starving U.S. and Filipino troops died on their way into captivity in what became known as the Bataan Death March.

A captured Japanese Army photograph shows U.S. soldiers arriving at a Philippine prison camp after the infamous Bataan Death March. *(Library of Congress)*

In the spring of 1942, Americans got some good news. In April, U.S. air force colonel James "Jimmy" Doolittle, flying off an aircraft carrier, led 16 B-25

Dauntless SBD-3 dive-bombers from the carrier USS *Hornet* attack the Japanese battleship *Mikuma* on the afternoon of June 6, 1942, during the Battle of Midway. *(Library of Congress)*

"I shall return."

—General Douglas MacArthur, after escaping from the Japanese invasion of the Philippines

bombers on a raid against Japan. In May, planes from U.S. and Japanese carriers clashed in the Battle of the Coral Sea north of Australia. Although the U.S. Navy lost the carrier USS *Lexington,* the Japanese force suffered the loss of two carriers, two destroyers, and many other ships. This battle halted the advance of Japanese naval forces to the south.

In June, a Japanese force based around four carriers tried to capture U.S.-held Midway Island, about 1,200 miles south of Hawaii. By this time, U.S. Navy codebreakers had cracked Japan's military codes, so naval commanders knew the attack was coming. In the battle that followed, U.S. planes sank all four Japanese carriers.

After the Battle of Midway, Japan was on the defensive. The Japanese still held many Pacific islands, and they were determined to hold them at all costs.

In August 1942, U.S. Marines landed on Guadalcanal, in the Solomon Islands of the South Pacific. For four months, the Marines (later joined by U.S. Army troops) fought the Japanese in the island's steaming jungles, while U.S. and Japanese warships clashed in a series of battles offshore.

In February 1943, the last of the Japanese defenders were driven from Guadalcanal. At the same time, U.S. Army troops fought an equally hard campaign to drive the Japanese from the large island of New Guinea, north of Australia.

These battles set the pattern for the island war in the South Pacific. Conditions for the fighting men were miserable. Tropical diseases, including malaria felled more men than combat. The fighting was savage and

While his buddies look on, medics treat a wounded man on Guadalcanal. *(Library of Congress)*

OKLAHOMA OK!

March 31, 1943, marked a new high point in a uniquely U.S. art form, the Broadway musical. On that night, at the St. James Theater in New York City, the curtain went up for the first performance of *Oklahoma!*, a musical by Richard Rodgers and Oscar Hammerstein II. Set in Oklahoma Territory in the early 1900s, before it became a state, *Oklahoma!*'s romantic story and beautiful songs appealed to theatergoers longing to escape from the worries of the wartime world and enjoy, for a few hours, a happier, simpler time. *Oklahoma!* got rave reviews and ran for 2,212 performances. It was also the first musical to have its entire musical score released on records.

This poster advertised the original 1943 production of *Oklahoma!* (Library of Congress)

often hand-to-hand. The Japanese fought to the last man and usually preferred suicide to capture. The Japanese were a formidable foe, but Guadalcanal, New Guinea, and campaigns on other islands proved they could be beaten.

WASHINGTON AT WAR

Organizing the people, industry, and resources of the United States to defeat the Axis powers was now the federal government's most important job. President Roosevelt tackled the job with the same energy he had shown in fighting the depression. As he had in the New Deal, Roosevelt set up several new government agencies. The most important agency was the War Production Board (WPB), created in January 1942.

At first, the transition from making consumer goods (such as cars and refrigerators) to military goods (such as tanks and rifles) was not an easy one for U.S. industry. There was too little cooperation between businesses, and between industry and the government.

As a result, Roosevelt established the WPB as a single agency with the power to direct the nation's economy during the war. Many of the WPB's members were wealthy businessmen. Because they donated their services to the government for a salary of $1, they were popularly known as "dollar-a-year-men."

One of the WPB's biggest jobs was setting priorities for war production in which WPB leaders decided which weapons and supplies were most important to the war effort. The WPB also divided up resources, such as oil, rubber, and steel, according to these priorities. For example, if the WPB decided that it was more important to produce aircraft carriers than tanks, it had the power to order steel mills to send their steel to shipyards rather than tank factories. In addition, the WPB decided which factories had to switch to war production and which could continue making goods for sale to civilians.

W. H. Harrison, director of the War Production Board (WPB), left, meets with his boss, WPB Chairman Donald M. Nelson. *(Library of Congress)*

The WPB also stopped or reduced the production of many civilian goods, such as cars and tires, to save resources for the war effort. This meant that even though Americans had more money in their pockets thanks to the booming wartime economy, there were fewer goods to spend it on. As a result, prices rose sharply—a condition known as inflation.

To control inflation, the federal government established another agency in 1942, the Office of Price Administration (OPA). The OPA tried to keep down inflation by setting maximum prices for many goods. Prices continued to rise during the war, but they would have risen much higher and caused much more hardship for people without the OPA's efforts.

PAYING FOR THE WAR: BONDS AND TAXES

Fighting the war was expensive. In 1940, the federal government spent about $9 billion; in 1945 it spent nearly 10 times that amount, most of it on the war effort. The government financed much of this amount

One of the worst home-front tragedies of the war years took place on November 28, 1942, when fire swept the Cocoanut Grove nightclub in Boston, Massachusetts, killing 492 people.

Ration books were composed of coupons that enabled users to purchase scarce materials such as gasoline and tires. They were treated like cash and were even more valuable in some ways—cash alone could not buy new tires.

by selling war bonds. By purchasing a war bond, the buyer loaned a sum of money to the U.S. Treasury. When the bond came due years later, the treasury paid the sum back to the buyer, plus interest. The price of the bonds ranged from $25 to $10,000.

To spur bond sales, the government published patriotic posters and sponsored bond drives featuring celebrities such as movie stars and military heroes. Workers joined programs in which part of their wages went toward buying bonds. Community groups, schools, and businesses chipped in to buy bonds, too. By the end of the war Americans had bought $36 billion worth of war bonds. Despite the success of war bonds, they covered only about half of the cost of the war. To bring in more money, the federal government raised taxes and introduced new kinds of taxes.

One of these new taxes was the so-called withholding tax. When the government raised taxes in 1942, millions of Americans who were not paying income tax now had to do so. It was up to individuals, however, to figure out how much they owed and to send the money to the government. It was a clumsy system and it brought in less money than the government had counted on.

In 1943, New York businessman Beardsley Ruml came up with the idea of a withholding or pay-as-you-go system. Under Ruml's system, taxes were automatically

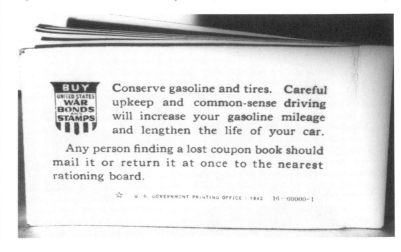

A ration book from 1944 reminds American civilians of the benefits of wise automobile use. *(Library of Congress)*

E FOR EXCELLENCE

Just as the U.S. Army and Navy had medals and other decorations to reward exceptional bravery in combat, civilian workers in World War II had a special honor to recognize exceptional service on the homefront. This was the Army-Navy E Certificate. (The E stood for excellence.) The federal government awarded the E certificate to companies that went "above and beyond the call of duty" in wartime production. Companies awarded the E Certificate hung a special red, white, and blue pennant in their factories or other facilities. The government presented about 4,000 E Certificates during the war.

taken out of a worker's paycheck. It was now up to the employer, not the employee, to send the correct amount of tax got to the government.

The new tax system was a major change in the daily lives of millions of Americans. The system continued after the war, and today most Americans pay the majority of their taxes this way.

INDUSTRY GOES INTO HIGH GEAR

It took World War II to finally end the depression that had plagued the United States for more than a decade. Wartime industries created more than 17 million jobs from 1941 to 1945. In a short period of time, the United States went from being a nation in which millions of people were looking for work to a nation in which anyone who wanted a job could find one.

Thanks to the wartime boom, Americans were also making more money than ever before. In 1940, the average pay for a skilled factory worker was about $25 per week. By 1944, the average weekly pay was about $45.

There was a big gap in pay, however, between skilled and unskilled workers. Almost one U.S. worker in four, for example, earned less than a dollar per hour during the war years.

Millions of Americans moved during the war years, sometimes several times, as workers sought jobs in

Women working in a war plant were urged by the government to wear their hair short or to wear scarves to keep it from catching in machinery. *(Franklin D. Roosevelt Presidential Library and Museum)*

wartime industries. Many people moved to the West Coast states—California, Washington, and Oregon—which were home to many shipyards and aircraft plants. About 8 million Americans moved to the West Coast in the 1940s—one of the biggest migrations in U.S. history. Large industrial cities such as Detroit and Chicago also attracted hundreds of thousands of workers, many from the rural South.

Making a new life in a new community was often difficult for wartime workers and their families. Housing was in short supply in many towns and cities. Families set up housekeeping wherever they could, sometimes living in garages and converted chicken coops. Some landlords raised rents on houses and apartments in an effort to make fast money from the newcomers. The OPA responded by controlling rents in some areas, but like the fight to control inflation, the agency was not completely successful.

Families also had to worry about childcare. With both parents often working long hours, many children and teenagers were left on their own after school. Some defense plants set up child-care centers for their workers, but most did not. First Lady Eleanor Roosevelt tried to interest the federal government in setting up a national day-care system without success. The need for workers also led as many as a million high-school students to drop out of school and take jobs during the war years.

WOMEN IN THE WARTIME WORKFORCE

With so many men in uniform, it was not long before women began to take their place on assembly lines and shop floors across the country. At first, however, women workers had to overcome the same prejudicial attitudes faced by the first women to join the military. Just as many military officers believed that women did not have

the necessary qualities to serve in uniform, many business owners believed that women did not have the strength and stamina for jobs in heavy industries. For example, while more than 750,000 women applied for jobs in wartime plants in the months after Pearl Harbor, only about 80,000 were actually hired. Soon, however,

ROSIE THE RIVETER

The May 29, 1943, cover of the *Saturday Evening Post* magazine featured a painting by the artist Norman Rockwell. The painting showed a strong woman factory worker on her lunch break, balancing a riveting gun on her lap. This famous painting became known as Rosie the Riveter—a name that had first appeared in a 1942 song celebrating women workers. (After the song was released, Americans learned there was at least one real-life Rosie the Riveter—Rose Will Monroe, who worked in a Ford aircraft plant in Michigan.) Rockwell's painting was so popular that the original artwork toured the country to promote the sale of war bonds. Rosie the Riveter quickly came to symbolize the millions of U.S. women workers.

Another real-life Rosie the Riveter worked at the Mare Island Shipyard in San Francisco. *(Library of Congress)*

THE AUTOMOBILE IN WARTIME

The U.S. love affair with the car is well known. But during World War II, Americans had to put their car cravings on hold as cars, automotive parts, tires, and gasoline were among the most tightly rationed products.

Car companies stopped producing cars for the civilian market and started rolling out aircraft instead. Ford made B-24s; General Motors made B-25s; and Chrysler made B-26s. Only a small number of civilians could purchase new cars after 1942. Even police forces could not purchase any new patrol car without proving that it would replace a pre-1937 model that had more than 100,000 miles on it.

Gasoline ration coupons were extremely valuable. They were not all equivalent: Five levels of gasoline rationing existed, and coupons were labeled from A to E. The A coupons, which could be used to buy gasoline for driving for pleasure, entitled the bearer to purchase three to five gallons per week. However, A tickets were discontinued in 1943. B tickets were reserved for commuters, who were allowed the most purchases per week.

Gasoline rationing did cut down on driving and meant that Americans had to carpool, or share rides. One dramatic poster from the Office of War Information stated: "When you ride alone, you ride with Hitler! Join a car-sharing club today!" Other posters urged every American to consider, "Is Your Trip Necessary?"

African-American labor leader A. Philip Randolph was photographed in November 1942. *(Library of Congress)*

the need for workers made business owners change their minds.

U.S. women worked jobs that few women, if any, had ever done before: welding steel plate in shipyards, operating machine tools in weapons plants, and fitting machine guns into fighter planes in aircraft factories. By the end of the war, about 3.5 million women worked in wartime industries—more than a third of the total defense workforce.

AFRICAN AMERICANS IN THE WARTIME WORKFORCE

Another group that faced discrimination were African-American workers. Before Pearl Harbor, the owners of many defense plants refused to hire African Americans. Prejudice was so widespread that A. Philip Randolph, head of the Brotherhood of Sleeping-Car Porters, the leading African-American labor union, called for a 100,000-person protest march in Washington, D.C.

In response, President Roosevelt issued Executive Order 8802 on June 25, 1941. The order outlawed "discrimination because of race, creed, color, or national origin" in hiring in the defense industry. The order also set up another federal agency, the Fair Employment Practice Committee (FEPC), to investigate cases of discrimination against African Americans in wartime industries

For many African Americans, wartime work offered a way out of the poverty and prejudice they faced in the South. About 700,000 African Americans left the southern states during the war years, mostly for the West Coast and the North. Michigan's African-American population more than doubled in the 1940s. California's grew by more than 200 percent.

> As more and more women entered the industrial workforce, clothing manufacturers reported in 1942 that sales of women's trousers rose by 500 percent over 1941 levels.

LABOR IN WARTIME

In 1940, about 8 million U.S. workers belonged to labor unions—approximately a quarter of the workforce. A week after Pearl Harbor, the leaders of the American Federation of Labor (AFL), the largest single labor union, pledged not to lead any strikes until the war was over. For the most part, the pledge was kept.

One big exception occurred in early 1943, when John L. Lewis, head of the United Mine Workers union (UMW) led 500,000 coal miners on a strike for higher

THE PORT CHICAGO MUTINY

On July 17, 1944, two ships carrying ammunition exploded along the docks at Port Chicago, California. More than 300 sailors were killed and another 390 injured, most of them African Americans. When the stunned survivors were ordered back to work unloading ships just a few weeks later, they refused, believing that conditions were still unsafe and that they were at risk of another explosion. The navy responded by holding a courtmartial that found 50 African-American sailors guilty of mutiny. The convicted men, however, were not given a real chance to defend themselves in court. They remained in prison until President Harry Truman ordered them freed in 1946. However, they were still considered guilty of mutiny. A campaign to clear their names is still underway.

NYLON, THE MIRACLE FIBER

There were no pantyhose in 1940. Women wore stockings, one for each leg, held up with garters attached to a belt worn under their clothes. The best hose were knitted of silk, on complex machines, and sewn together with a tiny seam in the back. But silk sagged, was rather thick and opaque, and took a very long time to dry after washing.

The Du Pont chemical company had developed nylon and introduced it to the public on October 28, 1938. Their press release claimed: "Though wholly fabricated from such common raw materials as coal, water and air, nylon can be fashioned into filaments strong as steel, as fine as the spider's web, yet more elastic than any of the common natural fibers and possessing a beautiful luster." Du Pont specifically intended the consumer material for women's hose. The name came from New York (ny) and London (lon), two cities where Du Pont thought the item would be particularly popular.

But women everywhere went wild for the new nylon stockings, which lasted longer, looked more attractive, and fit better than silk. When nylon stockings first went on sale, in May 1940, stores nationwide sold out immediately. But to many women's horror, the hose were suddenly snatched away. The War Production Board decreed that all nylon production had to be devoted to the war effort, for parachutes and tires. Silk, too, was used for parachutes and was in short supply.

One woman wrote in an October 1942 issue of *Business Week* magazine: "Women were given a glorified hose several yeas ago, and that is what they want now. Nylon hose came, conquered and disappeared with a short time and now the women are rebelling good and strong . . . These substitutes which are being thrust upon us this fall are horrible, last no time and certainly don't look as good as nylon."

A thriving black market existed for nylon stockings, but because the only legitimate buyer of nylon was the U.S. government, most items on the black market were fakes. Many women wound up paying $10 a pair for cheap, inferior rayon stockings labeled "nylon" or using eyeliner to draw a mock seam on the back of their bare legs.

To save electricity for the war effort, the United States adopted Daylight Savings Time— originally called "War Time" when it began in 1942— across the nation. Clocks were set one hour ahead of Standard Time on February 9.

pay. President Roosevelt responded swiftly by putting the nation's coal mines under government control. The miners went back to work in May. In June, Congress later passed the Smith-Connally Anti-Strike Act, which outlawed strikes in any industry that was important to the war effort.

Labor leaders were unhappy about some government policies, including the April 1943 wage freeze. This act kept most workers' pay at its present level in an effort to control wartime inflation. However, prices continued to go up slightly. In the words of one union official, the policy "freezes wages but permits . . . a continued rise in the cost of living."

The federal government worked hard to keep up good relations between business and labor for the sake of the war effort. This was the job of the National War

Labor Board (NWLB), which was founded in January 1942. The 12-member board included representatives of labor, business, and the government. Throughout the war, the NWLB settled conflicts between unions and business owners and set government policy toward labor. By the war's end, union membership had increased to more than 11 million workers, and a third of all U.S. workers belonged to a union.

FEEDING A WORLD AT WAR

The wartime work of U.S. farmers and ranchers was just as important as that of defense workers. Besides feeding the civilian population and the enlisted men and women overseas, U.S. farms helped feed the nation's allies. Between March 1941 and July 1944, the United States sent more than $2 billion worth of meat, grain, and other foods to Britain, and about $1 billion worth to the Soviet Union. The amount of food produced during World War II was more than a third higher than in 1935–1939.

U.S. farms faced a labor shortage even more severe than the one faced by industry. Many farmers volunteered for the military or were drafted. Others moved to cities to take defense jobs. By the end of the war, the nation's farm population had fallen by 20 percent.

To keep crops growing, the governments of the United States and Mexico began the Bracero Program in August 1942. The program allowed Mexican citizens to enter the United States to work on farms for specific periods of time. (*Bracero* is a Spanish term meaning "hired laborer.") During the war years, hundreds of thousands of Mexican workers crossed the border to labor on farms in California and Texas and other southwestern states.

The Bracero Program provided much-needed farm labor, but some Braceros were overworked, underpaid, and sometimes mistreated by farm owners. The federal

"Food Is a Weapon of War—As Important as Guns and Ammunition!"
—Government poster, 1943

The WPB distributed this poster to war plants to urge workers to even greater levels of production. *(Library of Congress)*

Farm Security Administration (FSA) managed the program, but the FSA did not have enough money or staff to make sure all the Braceros were treated fairly.

By the time the war ended, many farm owners had come to depend on Bracero labor, so the program continued in peacetime. More than 3 million Braceros worked in the United States between 1942 and the end of the program in 1964.

THE PRODUCTION MIRACLE

Once U.S. industry got into high gear, the results were awesome. Between July 1940 and August 1945, U.S. plants, factories, and shipyards turned out almost 300,000 aircraft; more than 76,000 ships; 2.5 million tanks, trucks, and other vehicles; more than 20 million rifles, machine guns, and other weapons, and more than 40 billion rounds of ammunition. By the war's end, the United States was supplying half of all the weapons used by the Allies.

U.S. industry not only produced vast amounts of military hardware but also produced them with amazing speed as the war went on. In 1941, for example, it took almost a year to build a cargo ship. By 1943, shipyards had cut the time to one month, and one particular ship was built in five days.

Without this mighty effort, the road to victory would have been much longer and many more Allied lives would have been lost. World War II was won in U.S. factories and farms as well as on the battlefield.

CHAPTER 4

HARD FIGHTING AND HIGH SPIRITS, 1943–1944

I N THE SECOND PART OF PRESIDENT Roosevelt's third term, the war dominated life in the United States. War news dominated newspapers and the news programs on radio, as well as most Americans' minds and hearts. Nearly every American knew a soldier or was affected by the wartime economy, rationing, or manufacturing. The news from all fronts—in the Pacific, Europe, and Africa—was breathlessly awaited.

Troops of the U.S. Army's 93rd Division on patrol in the thick jungle of Bougainville in the South Pacific in May 1943. *(Library of Congress)*

The challenges of amphibious (land-sea) warfare led U.S. military engineers to develop the DUKW—a 2.5-ton truck vehicle that could swim ashore from landing craft carrying 25 troops, and then serve as a truck on land.

ISLAND-HOPPING IN THE PACIFIC, LANDINGS IN THE MEDITERRANEAN

In the Pacific War against Japan, U.S. commanders adopted a strategy called island-hopping. Instead of attacking Japanese strongholds head-on, U.S. forces tried to go around them to seize other islands that were not as heavily defended. These islands would serve as bases for further advances, so U.S. forces moved ever closer to Japan.

After the victories on Guadalcanal and New Guinea, U.S. forces began landing on islands in the Central Pacific. In East Asia, U.S. troops joined British, Indian, and Chinese troops fighting the Japanese in Burma (now Myanmar), and helped the Chinese armies struggling to hold back the invading Japanese.

While U.S. forces pushed back the Japanese in the Pacific, the United States took the first steps against Germany and Italy. On November 8, 1942, British and U.S. troops commanded by U.S. general Dwight D. Eisenhower landed on the North African coast. Because France had made peace with Germany, some French troops fought the Allies as they came ashore. Other French soldiers welcomed the Allies. The landings were successful.

By this time, bombers from the U.S. Eighth Air Force, based in southern England, were bombing Germany in an effort to destroy its industries and transportation network, although their aircrews suffered heavy losses.

On July 10, 1943, an Allied invasion fleet began landing the first of 500,000 U.S. and British troops on the island of Sicily off the southern coast of Italy. The Allies conquered Sicily on August 16, but many German troops escaped to the Italian mainland.

While the fighting raged in Sicily, the war-weary Italian government overthrew the nation's dictator, Benito Mussolini, and tried to make peace with the Allies. There were hundreds of thousands of German troops in Italy, however, who quickly occupied the country.

In early September, the Allies invaded the mainland of Italy. The Allied advance toward Rome, Italy's capital, was slow and costly. Rome did not fall to the Allies until June 5, 1944, and fighting in northern Italy continued until the end of the war in Europe.

LIFE ON THE HOME FRONT

Back in the United States, Americans of all kinds and ages did whatever they could to support the soldiers, sailors, and airmen fighting around the world. There were plenty of opportunities for civilians to join the war effort. One way was to become a Civil Defense volunteer. Organized by the federal government's Office of Civilian Defense (OCD), these volunteers worked in their

"Casualties many; Percentage of dead not known; Combat efficiency; we are winning."

—Marine Corps Colonel David Shoup during the Battle of Tarawa in the Pacific, November 1943

A U.S. supply ship explodes off Sicily after a direct hit from a German bomber. *(Library of Congress)*

"Maybe I can be funny after the war, but nobody who has seen this war can be funny about it while it's going on. The only way I can try to be a little bit funny is to make something out of the humorous situations which come up even when you don't think life could be any more miserable."

—G.I. cartoonist Bill Mauldin

communities to guard against enemy air raids. Aircraft spotters spent many hours on rooftops scanning the skies for signs of enemy aircraft. Air-raid wardens made sure that people kept their curtains drawn during blackout drills, so that no light escaped to guide enemy bombers to their targets.

Other U.S. men and women volunteered their time to the Red Cross. Red Cross volunteers prepared bandages for first-aid kits; visited wounded servicemen in hospitals, distributed magazines, coffee, and other small comforts to soldiers headed overseas, and collected blood for the wounded.

Civil Defense workers and other volunteers also organized scrap drives to collect metal, rubber, paper, and other materials that could be recycled into weapons and other materials for the war effort. All over the country, people turned in old shoes, tin cans, newspapers, and an amazing variety of other objects. Families also saved grease from cooking, which was used to make explosives.

"Use it up, wear it out, make it do, or do without" was a popular saying during the war years. With half

COUPON CLIPPING

On May 4, 1942, War Ration Book No. 1 was distributed, composed of detachable one-inch-square coupons in red and blue. Within two weeks, more than 90 percent of Americans had registered.

Each four-person household received about 192 points, which could be used to buy controlled commodities such as butter, sugar, shortening, meat, and coffee. A four-person household—two adults and two children—got about two pounds of meat a week, about the same amount of meat as is found in an eight Quarter Pounders from McDonald's today.

During the week of April 24, 1942, the sale of sugar was totally prohibited, and it was strictly regulated afterward. Because food was rationed, children were urged to join the Clean Plate Club, eating every bit of food on their plate. Nothing could be wasted.

Some people bought and sold commodities outside the system. This was known as the black market. When someone said, "I bought that coffee from Mr. Black," or "I'm going to get gas from Mr. Black," it meant they bought the items on the black market.

Despite the smiling faces in this photograph, shopping with ration stamps was often a confusing business for shopkeepers and shoppers alike. (*Franklin D. Roosevelt Presidential Library and Museum*)

"Home was where the family was, where the girlfriend lived, where the food was soft and the toilet was private. That was what we were fighting for."

—Alvin M. Josephy, marine in the Pacific

the country's industry working for the war effort, ordinary Americans had to adapt to many small changes in their daily lives. To save cloth, for example, the government encouraged changes in clothing styles, such as victory pants without cuffs and business suits without vests. To save paper, publishers produced paperback books instead of hardcovers, and printed pages with smaller margins and more text.

Children took part in the war effort, too. The Boy Scouts, Girl Scouts, and other groups led scrap drives and helped with civil-defense drills. School classes collected money for war bonds. With both parents working in many families, older children pitched in with household chores and looked after their younger brothers and sisters. The war affected children's lives in other ways. Comic-book heroes fought the Germans and Japanese. Toys were now made of paper and cardboard because metal and other materials were needed by the military.

Civil Defense Volunteers operated the War Emergency Radio Service, which maintained communications between hospitals, police and fire stations, and other emergency services. *(Library of Congress)*

RATIONING AND VICTORY GARDENS

The biggest change in Americans' daily lives came with the start of rationing in January 1942. Rationing meant limiting the purchase of many goods, including gasoline and many foods. The idea behind rationing was to make sure that all Americans got a fair share of the limited goods available, while keeping the military supplied with everything it needed.

Managed by the Office of Price Administration (OPA), rationing was applied through a system of ration books issued to every family or individual. The books were filled with color-coded stamps, each with a different point value. The OPA decided the point value of various goods. A pound of hamburger meat, for example, was worth seven points. When a shopper bought a pound of hamburger, he or she gave the store owner seven points' worth of stamps and the money to purchase the meat.

Sugar and coffee were the first foods to be rationed. Meat and dairy products, such as butter and cheese, soon followed. Americans learned to make do with substitutes, using ground soybeans in place of coffee and horsemeat in place of beef. Neither proved very popular. Nonfood items were rationed as well. A leather shortage, for example, led to the rationing of shoes.

For most Americans who were used to driving wherever they wanted to go, gasoline rationing was the hardest restriction to get used to. By mid-1942, a major gasoline shortage and the military's thirst for fuel led to the tight rationing of gas. With the exception of doctors,

In some communities, theaters gave free tickets to moviegoers who brought in metal or rubber items.
(Library of Congress)

SCHOOLCHILDREN AT WAR

Every American was eager to help the soldiers overseas. Schoolchildren participated in Red Cross drives, collecting material for bandages and putting together care packages for fighting men. They sold war bonds to friends and relatives, to raise money for the U.S. government, rather than selling candy or wrapping paper to raise money for their school programs.

Scrap drives were another way that civilians helped the war effort. Kids collected tin cans; adults collected scrap metal. Used lard and cooking grease were also needed. War Ration Book No. 4 told users: "When you have used your ration, salvage the Tin Cans and Waste Fats. They are needed to make munitions for our fighting men. Cooperate with your local Salvage Committee."

"Is this trip necessary?"

—Government slogan promoting gas rationing

> **C**attle rustling returned to the West during the war as gangs of black marketeers raided isolated ranches, quickly killing and slaughtering livestock and hauling the meat away for illegal sale.

truck drivers, and people in some other vital jobs, most U.S. drivers got only an A ration stamp for gas—enough for three gallons a week. New tires were not available either, because the Japanese had cut off the supply of rubber from Southeast Asia.

The government also stopped the production of new cars so auto factories could switch to making military vehicles, It also established a national speed limit of 35 miles per hour to save fuel. As a result of gas rationing, most people in wartime traveled on trains, which were often crowded.

Most Americans cheerfully accepted the complications of rationing and the shortages of various goods. After all, rationing was a small sacrifice compared to the hardships people were suffering in the other countries at war.

Some dishonest people, however, bought and sold scarce goods, especially meat and gas, outside the rationing system. This illegal system was known as the black market. Because rationing was so complicated, it was fairly easy to cheat, and the OPA did not have nearly enough inspectors to make sure that everyone followed

A teacher explains the rationing system to her class. Each member of the family received his or her own ration book.
(Library of Congress)

A family shows off their Victory garden harvest. *(Library of Congress)*

the system. Most of this illegal trading was on a small scale, but some black marketeers made fortunes.

Another big change in daily life was the arrival of Victory gardens. With most of the nation's farmers growing food for the war effort, the government encouraged people to grow their own vegetables. Americans responded by planting more than 20 million gardens, in vacant lots in the big cities and in backyards in the

V-MAIL

For most Americans, letters were the only way to keep in touch with loved ones in the service. So many letters were sent that their combined weight put a strain on shipping, so a new system, V-mail, was developed. (The V stood for "victory.") V-mail letters were written on a single sheet of paper that was then photographed, reduced in size, and then sent overseas or back home to the United States. Like newspaper reports or radio broadcasts, all V-mail bound for the United States was censored by officers to make sure the sender had not written anything that might be of use to the enemy. This censorship was not much liked by many enlisted men, as it meant that their officers got to read their most personal thoughts. (Officers censored each other's mail.) More than 55 million pieces of V-mail were sent between 1942 and 1945.

A 1944 poster promotes the use of V-Mail. The V-Mail system reduced the weight of the average letter by 98 percent. *(Library of Congress)*

THE ZOOT SUIT RIOTS

Clashes between different racial and ethnic groups were among the worst aspects of life in wartime America. In the summer of 1943, riots between whites and African Americans in New York City and Detroit left more than 40 people dead and hundreds injured. In Los Angeles, Mexican Americans were the targets of mob violence, especially teenagers. Their clothing, called zoot suits, consisted of flashy outfits with long jackets and narrow pegged-style pants. In the spring of 1943, there were several clashes between soldiers and sailors and the so-called zoot suiters. On June 3, sailors attacked a group of Mexican-American zoot suiters in revenge for a sailor who had been injured in an earlier fight. This fight led to a week of rioting that spread through several Los Angeles neighborhoods. In many cases, the police did not stop the servicemen, though they arrested more than 600 Mexican Americans, many of them simply for wearing a zoot suit. In her newspaper column, First Lady Eleanor Roosevelt wrote, "The question goes deeper than just suits. [Racial prejudice] is a problem with roots going a long way back, and we do not always face these problems as we should."

A soldier checks out a couple of civilians wearing zoot suits at a 1942 dance. The flashy outfits were a favorite of jazz fans. *(Library of Congress)*

suburbs. By the end of the war, Americans were growing about a third of all the vegetables they ate.

Many Americans would remember some aspects of the war years fondly. It was a time when the country was united in a common cause. It was also a period of prosperity for many who had suffered poverty during the depression. The war years, however, were also a time of worry and sadness for millions of people. By 1945, nearly every family had at least one son, father, brother, or other relative in uniform. Even if a loved one was not in the combat zone, the war usually meant long years of separation. Families of men overseas lived in fear of a message from the War Department that began "We regret to inform you..." This opening meant a loved one had been wounded or captured or, even worse, was missing or had been killed.

REPORTERS, WRITERS, AND THE WAR

With television a new invention and the internet decades away, Americans of the 1940s got their news from the radio, magazines, and newspapers. During the war, about 500 broadcasters, reporters, and photographers accompanied U.S. forces overseas. Although these war correspondents carried typewriters and cameras instead of weapons, they shared much of the same hardship and danger as the soldiers they followed into action.

The best known correspondent of the war was Indiana-born Ernie Pyle. In his reports from the front in North Africa and Europe, Pyle wrote movingly about the experiences of ordinary fighting men. When he was killed in action in the Pacific late in the war, millions of Americans, in uniform and out, mourned him. Several famous novelists of the time, including Ernest Hemingway and John Steinbeck, also served as war correspondents.

Not all the correspondents were men. Margaret Bourke-White, a photographer for *Life* magazine, photographed the war in Europe, including the bombing campaign against Germany. Journalist Martha Gellhorn was one of the first correspondents to report from Normandy, France, during the D-Day invasion.

The armed services had their own newspapers and magazines, including the army's *Stars and Stripes*, written by servicemen and women. Among the Stars and Stripes' most popular features were the cartoons of a young sergeant named Bill Mauldin.

Women correspondents were officially barred from the D-Day landings, but Martha Gellhorn stowed away in disguise to get her story. *(Library of Congress)*

CASABLANCA: THE MOVIE

History met Hollywood head-on in November 1942 when *Casablanca* opened in U.S. theaters. The movie starred Humphrey Bogart and Ingrid Bergman as lovers in the North African city during the time it was controlled by the pro-German French government. The romantic story of love set against a background of war made the movie a huge hit, and it is considered one of the greatest movies of all time. The film's popularity got a boost because it was released in late November 1942, just weeks after the Allied invasion of North Africa, which included landings not far from Casablanca.

FROZEN FOOD COMES OF AGE

Clarence Birdseye developed technology for successfully freezing foods in the 1920s. His Birdseye company had introduced frozen vegetables, meats, and fish in 1930. But it was the shortage of tin cans during World War II that helped make frozen food popular and accepted by U.S. consumers.

The Japanese conquest of the South Pacific and Southeast Asia made tin hard to obtain, and the War Production Board limited the amount of tin that canneries could use for the civilian market. But frozen foods could be packaged in paper, cellophane, and cardboard, all of which remained available throughout the war.

Grocers, who had been reluctant to stock frozen food because of the expense of preserving it, suddenly found that canned goods were in short supply. As a result, stores installed refrigerators, and consumers were exposed to a wide range of frozen goods.

According to the National Frozen and Refrigerated Food Association, the most successful frozen product of the 1940s was frozen concentrated orange juice from Minute Maid, followed by Mrs. Paul's fish sticks. These items can still be found in supermarket freezers in the 21st century.

HOLLYWOOD GOES TO WAR

Going to the movies was the most popular form of entertainment for Americans in the 1940s. During the war years, about 90 million people (two-thirds of the population) went to the movies at least once a week. The average ticket price was 35 cents in the 1940s.

After Pearl Harbor, Hollywood mobilized for the war effort in the same way that U.S. industry did. The major movie studios (Twentieth Century Fox, Metro-Goldwyn-Mayer [MGM], Paramount Pictures, RKO Studios, Warner Brothers, Columbia Pictures, United Artists, and Universal Pictures) worked closely with the federal government's Office of War Information (OWI) and the Bureau of Motion Picture Affairs.

The OWI advised the studios as to the kind of movies they should make. The idea was to use the power of the movies to keep the country united against Germany and Japan and to inspire Americans to even greater efforts in supporting the war. As a result, wartime movies usually depicted German and Japanese characters as evil monsters, while U.S. and Allied characters were almost always noble and brave.

Naturally, the war inspired many movies. Some films were based on real events, but with added drama and romance. The movie *Thirty Seconds Over Tokyo*,

The Hollywood movie studios went to great efforts to send prints of new films overseas for the enjoyment of G.I. audiences. In some cases, servicemen and servicewomen saw the latest releases before they debuted in American theaters.

KING OF THE CROONERS

Some male singers of the time were called crooners because of the distinctive way in which they sang into the microphone. The most popular crooner was a skinny young man from Hoboken, New Jersey, named Frank Sinatra. After singing with the Harry James and Tommy Dorsey big bands, Sinatra went solo in 1942. His most devoted fans were teenaged girls, a group often called bobbysoxers because of the short socks that were then in fashion, due partly to a wartime shortage of stockings. When Sinatra performed at New York's Paramount Theater in the spring of 1942, newspapers reported that the audience screamed so loudly that Sinatra's singing could barely be heard. Several young women also fainted. Sinatra was less popular with young men serving overseas: The teen idol did not have to serve in the military because of an ear condition.

Danny Kaye had just become a Broadway star in 1939. Although his career was taking off, he still took time to appear on USO tours. *(Library of Congress)*

Frank Sinatra signs up for the draft in 1943—thanks to a punctured eardrum, however, he was never called up for service. *(Library of Congress)*

THE SLINKY, THE SLINKY: A WONDERFUL TOY

Military engineering often spins off products that prove useful to civilian industry and make everyday life easier. But although Richard James's invention did neither, it quickly became an American icon. Richard and Betty James invented the Slinky.

In 1943, Richard James was a naval engineer, developing new types of springs. When he knocked a few springs over by accident, he saw how they seemed to walk down an incline and then topple down steps.

He and his wife Betty worked with the springs, trying out many different sizes and materials. Betty named the final product the Slinky, and together they sold 400 of the first Slinkys to Gimbel's department store in Philadelphia. Within two hours of putting Slinkys on the shelves, the store sold out all their stock, and the Jameses rushed to produce more Slinkys. Children and adults have been delighted by the toy ever since.

which tells the story of the Doolittle Raid, stars Spencer Tracy as Colonel Jimmy Doolittle. *The Flying Tigers,* starring John Wayne, is about the U.S. pilots who helped China fight back against the Japanese invaders.

In addition to these wartime dramas, there were plenty of other movies to take Americans' minds off the war for a while. Walt Disney's full-length animated movie, *Bambi,* was among the most popular films of the war years. Americans laughed at the antics of comedy duos, including Bob Hope and Bing Crosby, and Bud Abbott and Lou Costello. Moviegoers sang along with splashy musicals such as *Yankee Doodle Dandy* (featuring James Cagney as songwriter George M. Cohan), and *Meet Me in St. Louis* (starring Judy Garland).

Some movie stars volunteered for military service. The U.S. Army Air Force (USAAF), considered the most glamorous of the armed services, was especially popular with actors. Actor and future president Ronald Reagan served in the USAAF, although he was never sent overseas. Another movie star, Jimmy Stewart, joined the USAAF as an enlisted man. He rose to the rank of colonel and survived many dangerous missions.

Hollywood stars also went on war bond drives, touring the country to urge Americans to buy more bonds. Actress Carole Lombard lost her life in a 1942 plane crash while on a bond drive. Her husband, the popular actor Clark Gable, served in the USAAF.

Movie star (and future president) Ronald Reagan poses with his first wife Jane Wyman, who was also a Hollywood star, in 1943. *(Library of Congress)*

Movie stars, musicians, and other performers also served in the United Services Organization (USO), which put on shows and sponsored dances to entertain U.S. servicemen and servicewomen around the world, even close to the front lines. In another reflection of the times, USO events were segregated, and African-American entertainers, including Lena Horne, performed for African-American servicemen.

Several famous movie directors joined the military and made documentary films. These nonfiction movies gave Americans at home a more realistic view of the war than the dramas made in Hollywood. John Ford's *The Battle of San Pietro,* for example, depicted the bitter fighting in Italy, and William Wyler's *Memphis Belle* followed the crew of a B-17 bomber on a mission from England to Germany.

Frank Capra, best known for his comedies before the war, directed a series of seven documentaries, the first of which appeared in 1943. Entitled *Why We Fight,* the series aimed to show Americans why the United States was in the war, and why an Allied victory was the only hope for a safe and peaceful future.

Trumpeter John Birks "Dizzy" Gillespie worked with the leading bands of the day before teaming up with saxophonist Charlie Parker in the mid-1940s to create the energetic bebop sound. *(Library of Congress)*

WARTIME MUSIC

During the war years the big band or swing sound was all the rage in popular music. Led by instrumentalists, such as trumpeter Harry James and clarinetist Benny Goodman, the big bands played a bright, up-tempo style of jazz that was perfect for dancing. The bands also featured female singers such as the Andrews Sisters. Trombonist Glenn Miller led one of the most popular bands of the time. Although Miller was old enough to avoid military service, he volunteered for the U.S. Army Air Force. Miller's Army Air Force Orchestra played at military bases and performed on the military's radio station, the Armed Forces Network. In December 1944, Miller flew from Britain to arrange a concert in newly

"I, like every patriotic American, have an obligation to fulfill. That obligation is to lend as much support as I can to winning the war."

—Glenn Miller, 1942

The Andrews Sisters—Patty, Maxine, and LaVerne—were among the most popular singers of the war years. Their heads appear above that of Harriet Hilliard in this poster. They also appeared in several wartime movies, including 1944's *Swingtime Johnny*. (Library of Congress)

In 1944, the first issue of *Seventeen* magazine was published by William Randolph Hearst's magazine division. Despite the ongoing war, high school girls were still interested in boys, dating, and the latest clothes.

liberated Paris. His plane vanished over the English Channel and presumably crashed into the sea.

Popular songs reflected the feelings of a nation at war. There were patriotic songs, including "Praise the Lord and Pass the Ammunition," and songs that poked fun at the enemy, such as "Der Fuhrer's Face." (*Der Fuhrer,* which means "the leader" in German, was one of Adolf Hitler's titles.) But there were also many songs that spoke of the pain of being separated from loved ones and the longing to be home again, such as "We'll Meet Again" and "You'd Be So Nice to Come Home to."

Americans had to get most of their music from the radio or concerts during the war years. At the time, recorded music was sold on records or albums. These records were made of shellac, a material imported from the East Indies, which Japan occupied. As a result, the recording industry released few records after Pearl Harbor. Many of the records released were special V-Disks, which were made to be sent to the troops overseas rather than for Americans at home. (V stood for Victory, and the letter was often used to mark items that were intended for or connected to the war effort.)

Big-band music was the most popular during the war, but in New York City nightclubs, African-American musicians, such as saxophonist Charlie Parker and trumpeter Dizzy Gillespie, pioneered a daring new style of jazz. This music was called bebop, which featured smaller bands and required fast, complicated improvisation. The new style of jazz, along with other African-American musical traditions, would soon change U.S. popular music forever.

CHAPTER 5

SWEEPING THROUGH EUROPE, 1944–1945

I N JUNE 1944, THE ALLIES BEGAN THE long-awaited invasion of Nazi-occupied northern Europe. During the early morning hours of June 6, airplanes dropped British and U.S. paratroopers behind the landing beaches on the Normandy coast in northern France. At around 6:30 A.M., landing craft began carrying the first of 156,000 Allied troops ashore. On most of beaches the troops landed safely and overwhelmed the German defenders. On other beaches there was fierce fighting and heavy casualties. By the end of the day, however, the beaches were secured.

U.S. troops go ashore from landing craft off the Normandy beaches. The D-Day operation involved 3,000 landing craft, 2,500 other ships, and almost 14,000 aircraft. *(Franklin D. Roosevelt Presidential Library and Museum)*

G.I.s prepare to board the landing craft that will put them ashore on a Normandy beach. Their M1 rifles are wrapped in plastic to protect them from water. *(Franklin D. Roosevelt Presidential Library and Museum)*

G.I.s catch a few minutes' rest in the Ardennes Forest during the Battle of the Bulge. *(Franklin D. Roosevelt Presidential Library and Museum)*

The invasion was a success, although it was not until the end of July that the Allied forces broke through the German forces inland and began advancing across France. By the end of August, the Allies had liberated Paris, France's capital, after more than four years of German occupation. During the same period of time, Soviet forces were pushing the Germans out of Russia and back into Poland and eastern Europe.

In December 1944, the Germans launched a last-ditch surprise attack against the British and U.S. forces, attacking through the Ardennes, a hilly, forested region in Belgium. The Germans fought their way through a section in the Allied line, creating a bulge that gave the fight its name, the Battle of the Bulge. The Germans retreated in January 1945, but they were pushed back. In the spring of 1945, the Allies crossed the Rhine River from the west and advanced deep into Germany, while from the east the Soviets surrounded and captured Berlin after a fierce campaign.

On April 30, Hitler committed suicide in Berlin. On May 7, the German army surrendered. The Allies proclaimed May 8, 1945, as V-E Day, for victory in Europe.

LOOKING TOWARD PEACE

In November 1944, while fighting raged around the world, Americans went to the polls to vote for president. The Democratic candidate was President Roosevelt, who was seeking a fourth term in office. The stress of leading the nation through the depression and the war had taken its toll on the president's health. His associates saw that he looked tired and sick, and some advisers urged him not to seek reelection. Roosevelt, however, was determined to see the war through to the end.

For his running mate, Roosevelt chose Missouri senator Harry S. Truman. The Republicans nominated New York governor Thomas E. Dewey. Roosevelt won the election and his fourth term.

In February 1945, Roosevelt traveled to Yalta in the southern Soviet region of Crimea to meet with British prime minister Winston Churchill and Soviet leader Joseph Stalin. At Yalta, these so-called Big Three decided on the shape of the postwar world. The leaders agreed to divide the soon-to-be-defeated Germany into four zones,

"Soldiers, Sailors, and Airmen . . . You are about to embark upon the Great Crusade."

—General Dwight Eisenhower's message to the Allied forces before D-Day

"Nuts!"

—U.S. General Anthony McAuliffe, answering a German call to surrender during the Battle of the Bulge

Hundreds of thousands of cheering people pack London's Trafalgar Square to celebrate V-E Day—the end of the war in Europe. *(Library of Congress)*

THE NAVAJO CODETALKERS

Keeping the enemy from eavesdropping on radio communications was a problem for the U.S. military in World War II. Radio messages were sent in code, but it took a long time to encode and decode messages, and there was always the chance the enemy would crack the code. In 1942, the Marine Corps came up with a unique technique to keep their front-line communications secure: using a code based on the language of the Native American Navajo nation. At that time there were only about 30 people who were not Navajo in the entire world who knew the language—and none of them were Japanese. During the war, about 400 Navajo Marines served as Codetalkers with Marine units in the Pacific. The Japanese never broke the code, and the Codetalkers played an important part in winning many battles in the Pacific, including Iwo Jima. Because the language did not have words to describe modern military equipment, the Codetalkers had to improvise. First, they cleverly adopted words from their language: The Navajo word *da-he-tih-hi,* which meant "hummingbird," was the code for "fighter plane," and *besh-lo,* which meant "iron fish," stood for "submarine." Second, they created a whole sophisticated code based around the Navajo alphabet. Codetalkers did much more than just talk Navajo to confuse spies.

In 1937 the Hormel Company introduced a canned pork-and-ham product—SPAM. During World War II, the company shipped some 100 million pounds of SPAM overseas to Allied forces and to hungry civilians in the war zones.

to be occupied by the United States, Britain, the Soviet Union, and France after the war. The Soviets agreed to join the war against Japan after the defeat of Germany, and to allow free elections in the central and eastern European countries it had freed from German occupation.

The Yalta Conference, however, also showed that the wartime alliance was starting to fall apart. Stalin supported a communist government in Poland, while the

President Franklin Roosevelt (center) was ill and exhausted when he arrived at the Yalta Conference in February 1945. *(Library of Congress)*

POLIO AND THE PRESIDENT

President Roosevelt liked to vacation at Warm Springs, Georgia, because he believed that swimming in the resort's waters helped his paralyzed legs. In 1921, when he was 41 years old, Roosevelt contracted polio, a crippling disease caused by a waterborne virus, after swimming at his family's vacation home on Campobello Island near New Brunswick, Canada. The disease left him paralyzed from the waist down. Roosevelt refused to let the disease hinder his political career. He built up the strength of his upper body through physical therapy until he was able to walk with leg braces and support from aides. Although his condition kept him in a wheelchair most of the time, reporters and photographers obeyed an unspoken agreement never to show him using a wheelchair. Most Americans were unaware of his disability throughout his 12-year presidency.

The most decorated U.S. soldier of the war war was Texan Audie Murphy. He won 37 medals, including the Medal of Honor for a singlehanded stand against German troops in France on January 26, 1945. He was just 20 years old at the time.

British and Americans supported other noncommunist Polish leaders. Stalin eventually got his way. The seeds of what would be called the cold war were being sown.

Sadly, President Roosevelt did not live to see the final victory. On April 12, 1945, the president died of a stroke while vacationing in Warm Springs, Georgia. At home and overseas, from the jungles of the Pacific to the front lines in Germany, Americans mourned the fallen president. Roosevelt had been in office since 1933. For many young Americans, he was the only president they had ever known.

The task of leading the nation now fell on President Harry Truman. Some Americans wondered if he was up to the job. Truman was not well known on the national scene until he became vice president. However, he proved to be a strong leader.

In August 1945, Truman went to the German city of Potsdam for the last big Allied conference of the war. By now only Stalin remained out of the original Big Three because Winston Churchill had been voted out of office as prime minister shortly after V-E Day. The new British prime minister, Clement Attlee, attended the conference. The Allied leaders agreed to fight together for

President Roosevelt's death saddened millions of people, not only in the United States but also around the world.
(New York Times)

The new U.S. president, Harry Truman (center), poses with the new British prime minister, Clement Attlee, and Joseph Stalin (right) at the Potsdam Conference in August 1945. *(Library of Congress)*

Japan's surrender, but once again there was much tension between the Soviet and the other Allied leaders.

VICTORY IN THE PACIFIC

In the Pacific, U.S. forces continued to island-hop ever closer to Japan. By mid-1944, U.S. forces had captured island airfields that put Japan within range of attack by U.S. aircraft. Carrying firebombs, U.S. B-29 bombers turned many Japanese cities into smoking ruins. In one raid, B-29s burned out 16 square miles of Tokyo. As many as 100,000 Japanese died in a single night of bombing.

In the South Pacific, General Douglas MacArthur carried out his promise to return to the Phillipines and free their people from Japanese occupation, starting with a landing at Leyte Gulf in October 1944. In the spring of 1945, U.S. forces seized the islands of Iwo Jima and Okinawa, although fierce Japanese resistance led to many U.S. casualties.

By this time Japan had lost almost all of the islands it had gained in 1941–42. Its cities were in ruins, its indus-

"I am more sorry for the people of this country and of the world than I am for ourselves."

—First Lady Eleanor Roosevelt after President Roosevelt's death

try was largely destroyed, and its population was nearly starving. Despite these facts, the Japanese government showed no sign of wanting to surrender, so Allied commanders began to plan the invasion of Japan itself.

The first landing in Japan was scheduled for November 1945. Given how fiercely the Japanese had fought in the Pacific, U.S. commanders believed that hundreds of thousands of Americans would be killed or wounded before Japan surrendered.

Fulfilling his promise to the Philippine people, General Douglas MacArthur wades ashore on the island of Leyte on October 25, 1944. *(Private Collection)*

Smoke rises from the ruins of Tokyo after the firebombing raid of March 9 and 10, 1945. *(Library of Congress)*

As head of the Office of Scientific Research and Development (OSRD), Vannevar Bush coordinated the efforts of more than 6,000 scientists working for the war effort. *(Library of Congress)*

SCIENCE AT WAR

Along with the military and industrial might of the United States, its science and technology also played a leading role in the Allied victory. Even before the United States entered World War II, the federal government realized that modern wars would be won in the laboratory as well as on the battlefield. In 1940, the government set up the National Defense Research Committee (NDRC) under the leadership of engineer and educator Vannevar Bush. A year later Bush became head of a second government agency, the Office of Scientific Research and Development (OSRD), while James B. Conant, president of Harvard University, directed the NDRC. These two agencies oversaw the efforts of universities and research laboratories across the country.

One wartime development that would affect daily life in the years to come was the electronic computer. Calculating machines of various kinds already existed, but the military needed faster and more powerful devices to crack enemy codes and to make weapons more accurate.

In 1944, engineers at Harvard University built the Mark I, one of the first computers. In contrast to today's computers, the Mark I was a huge machine. It was 55 feet long, eight feet high, and contained more than 760,000 parts. The University of Pennsylvania created an even bigger and more powerful computer, ENIAC (Electronic Numerical Integrator and Calculator). ENIAC was also the first computer to be fully electronic. (The Mark I used a combination of electronics and machinery to do its calculations.) The construction of ENIAC, however, was not completed until after the war's end.

Wartime needs also led to advances in medical technology that benefited both military and civilians. In earlier wars, many wounded soldiers died from infections. During World War II, penicillin came into widespread use for the first time. Penicillin was an antibiotic drug that fought bacterial infections

RAISING THE FLAG

Perhaps the best-known combat photograph of World War II shows six Marines raising the U.S. flag on February 23, 1945, on Mount Suribachi, the highest point on the island of Iwo Jima. Snapped by Associated Press photographer Joe Rosenthal, the picture is so perfect that some accused Rosenthal of posing the Marines. This is not entirely true. It is true, however, that the Marines were replacing a much smaller flag that had been planted a few hours before. (The rumor that it was planted the day before has been proven false.) The sight of the Stars and Stripes waving on the mountain brought cheers from the Marines on the beach. On a ship offshore, secretary of the Navy James Forrestal turned to General Holland Smith and said, "Holland, the raising of that flag on Suribachi means a Marine Corps for the next five hundred years." The battle for Iwo Jima was far from over, however, and by the time the island was secure, three of the six flag-raisers were dead.

throughout the body. Thanks to penicillin and similar drugs, tens of thousands of servicemen survived wounds that would otherwise have killed them.

Many lives were also saved by the new medical technology of blood transfusions. In 1940, an African-American scientist. Dr. Charles R. Drew, figured out a way to separate and store plasma (the liquid part of blood). Thanks to this advance, the Red Cross set up blood banks to store plasma and whole blood from civilian donors and sent the vital fluids to battlefronts.

The fight against malaria, a mosquito-borne tropical disease common in the Pacific, also resulted in medical breakthroughs. Before the war, a drug called quinine was used to prevent malaria. Quinine, however, comes from the bark of a tree (the cinchona) which was grown mostly in areas controlled by the Japanese. (Although the cinchona species originated in Central and South America, by the 1940s, 95 percent of all quinine came from what is today the Indonesian island of Java.) To make up for the lack of quinine, scientists developed a synthetic (artificial) anti-malaria drug called atabrine.

U.S. chemists also fought malaria by developing insecticides (chemicals that kill insects) to kill the mosquitoes carrying the disease. DDT, a leading insecticide, was sprayed widely in the Pacific. Back home, farmers began to use powerful chemicals to kill the insects that preyed on crops. Much later, many years after the

Although the bacteria-killing effect of penicillin was discovered in the 1920s, large stocks of the so-called wonder drug were not available until D-Day—just in time for the heaviest fighting in Europe. *(Library of Congress)*

AMAZING GRACE

One of the pioneering computer scientists of World War II was Grace Hopper. A professor of mathematics at Vassar College, Hopper joined the WAVES in 1943 and went to work at Harvard University's Computation Project, where she programmed the Mark I computer and its successor, the Mark II. After the war she worked for the Remington-Rand Corporation (later Sperry-Rand and today the Unisys Corporation), where she worked on COBOL, one of the leading computer-programming languages.

During this time she remained in the U.S. Navy Reserve, and she returned to active duty from 1967 to 1971. When she retired from the navy in 1986 with the rank of rear admiral, she was the oldest person serving in the U.S. military. By the time she died in 1992, the digital technology she had helped develop was a part of daily life for all Americans.

Grace Hopper is shown a few years before she was recalled to active duty in the U.S. Navy. *(Library of Congress)*

In the first postwar World Series, the American League's Detroit Tigers beat the National League's Chicago Cubs, four games to three.

war, people learned that DDT and other insecticides also caused damage to the environment.

Many of the technical advances of the war years came about because traditional materials were not available. When the Japanese conquest of the Dutch East Indies and the British Malay Islands (today the nations of Indonesia and Malaysia) cut off supplies of rubber, scientists developed synthetic rubber. Because so much metal was needed for the war effort, plastic (a by-product of oil) was used to make many products, from radios to furniture. Many people looked on plastic as a substitute for wood or metal, but after the war plastic came into greater use for a wider variety of products.

THE MANHATTAN PROJECT

The greatest scientific achievement of the war years was the secret program to build an atomic bomb. By the late 1930s, scientists understood that if the energy inside the atom could be released, a bomb far more powerful than any other could be made. In 1939, just before war broke out in Europe, the famous physicist Albert Einstein wrote a letter to President Roosevelt. Einstein warned of the danger that Germany might develop an atomic

BALLOON BOMBS

Unlike past wars, most of those killed in World War II were not military personnel but civilians. Bombings, hunger, and disease killed millions of people in the European nations; deaths were in the tens of millions in China and the Soviet Union. America was spared these horrible losses. Only six U.S. civilians died as a result of enemy action in the continental United States. The casualties were a woman and five children on a church-group fishing trip in Lakeview, Oregon, on May 5, 1945. The children found a shiny metal object in the woods that exploded when they tried to move it. The object was a small bomb that had crossed the Pacific Ocean from Japan beneath a balloon. The Japanese launched about 10,000 of these balloon bombs in an unsuccessful effort to start forest fires in the Pacific Northwest. In addition, at least one Japanese submarine launched a seaplane that dropped fire-bombs on an Oregon forest, which caused no damage.

On July 28, 1945, 13 people were killed and 26 injured when an air force bomber, which had lost its way in a heavy fog, crashed into New York City's Empire State Building—then the tallest building in the world.

weapon, and he urged the president to begin a U.S. atomic weapon program.

Research into the production of an atomic bomb began on a small scale in 1940, but after Pearl Harbor, the program became one of the government's top priorities. In June 1942, General Leslie Groves took command of the top-secret effort, which became known as the Manhattan Project.

Groves and his civilian scientific director, J. Robert Oppenheimer, gathered some of the best scientists in the country (many of them refugees from Europe) in Los Alamos, New Mexico, to work on the bomb. At the

THE BIRTH OF TUPPERWARE

Tupperware, so closely associated with the 1950s, was actually a product of advances in material technology in World War II. In 1938, salesman Earl Tupper founded the Tupper Plastics Company. Determined to be a millionaire, he spent much of World War II researching and developing new products and materials.

In 1945, he received some polyethylene, a new type of plastic, from the Du Pont chemical company. He combined it with his idea of a lid that can be sealed securely, modeled on the top of a paint can in reverse.

By the end of the decade, Tupper had patented the so-called burping seal on his line of food storage products and had begun to develop his sales force of housewives, who marketed the products from their home at Tupperware parties. The colored plastic containers in pastel tones and the parties themselves quickly became part of American popular culture.

THE LADIES' LEAGUE

Professional baseball continued during the war years, but because most of the best players were in the military, attendance at games dropped. In 1942, Philip K. Wrigley, owner of the Chicago Cubs, decided to form a women's league to keep people interested in baseball. The result was the All-American Girl's Professional Baseball League (AAGPBL), the professional league for women in the country. (The league actually played a combination of baseball and softball.) By the league's opening day in 1943, there were four teams: The Kenosha Comets and Racine Belles in Wisconsin, the Rockford Peaches in Illinois, and the South Bend Blue Sox in Indiana. Two more teams joined in 1944, after Wrigley sold the league: The Milwaukee Chicks (Wisconsin), and the Fort Wayne Daisies (Indiana). All in all, 600 women, including players from the United States, Canada, and Cuba, played in the AAGPBL. The league was very popular, with more than 650,000 people attending games in 1945. Many people expected the AAGPBL to go out of business after the male players came home from the war, but the league remained popular, adding even more teams and racking up a season attendance of almost a million in 1949. Eventually interest fell, however, and the AAGPBL teams played their last games in 1954. The story of the AAGPBL inspired the 1992 movie *A League of Their Own*.

The 1945 Rockford Peaches pose for a publicity shot. The team won the AAGPBL four times. *(National Baseball Hall of Fame Library and Museum)*

same time, Groves built two huge plants in Hanford, Washington, and Oak Ridge, Tennessee, to produce the radioactive material needed for the weapons.

The scientists at Los Alamos successfully exploded an atomic bomb in a secret test in the New Mexico desert on July 16, 1945. President Truman then gave the go-ahead to use the bomb against Japan.

On August 6, a B-29 bomber, the *Enola Gay,* took off from the island of Tinian and dropped an atomic bomb on the Japanese city of Hiroshima. The bomb carried the destructive power of 20,000 tons of regular explosive. Most of the city vanished in a single blinding flash. As many as 80,000 Japanese died instantly in Hiroshima. Tens of thousands died later from injuries or diseases caused by the radiation released by the bomb.

President Truman called on Japan to surrender or face "a rain of ruin from the air." Yet the Japanese government did not surrender. On August 9, the U.S. dropped a second atomic bomb on Nagasaki, killing about 40,000 people. Japan's emperor finally asked his government to seek peace.

News of Japan's surrender was announced on August 14— V-J Day. Americans went wild with joy. Huge crowds gathered everywhere, and strangers hugged and kissed.

Years later, some people questioned Truman's decision to use atomic weapons against Japan. There were those who felt it was wrong to use such a terrible weapon against civilians. Others believed that Japan would have surrendered soon even if the bombs had not been used.

At the time of the bombings, Americans were just happy that the war was over and that their loved ones

> *"It is my earnest hope that from this solemn occasion a better world shall emerge."*
>
> —General Douglas MacArthur at the Japanese surrender ceremony, September 2, 1945

> *"My God, what have we done?"*
>
> —*Enola Gay* co-pilot Robert Lewis

The distinctive mushroom cloud of an atomic explosion rises 60,000 feet into the air over Nagasaki on the morning of August 9, 1945. *(Library of Congress)*

After her husband's death, Eleanor Roosevelt worked with the United Nations to promote human rights. President Harry Truman called her "the First Lady of the World." *(Library of Congress)*

TOUGH TIMES, FUN FOOD

Despite the limits on consumer goods, some U.S. favorites went on sale for the first time in the 1940s, including Dairy Queen soft-serve frozen desserts and McDonald's hamburgers, developed from a combination of new food technology and consumers' demands for convenience.

Other new food products were just plain enjoyable, such as York Peppermint Patties, Cheerios (originally called Cheerioats), M&M's Plain Chocolate Candies, Junior Mints, and Kellogg's Raisin Bran. These items grew in popularity to become American icons, known all over the world.

would be coming home. For many people, however, there would be no joyful homecoming. The war claimed the lives of approximately 298,000 Americans. More than twice that number had been seriously wounded.

Compared to the rest of the world, the United States was fortunate. No one will ever know exactly how many people died in World War II, but it may be as many as 60 million. The war left millions more suffering and homeless. Besides the human cost, much of Europe and Asia lay in ruins.

The United States was now unquestionably the world's most powerful nation. It also possessed the world's most destructive weapons. Having played a leading role in winning the war, the United States now took the lead in shaping the postwar world.

On October 25, 1945, a new international organization came into being: the United Nations. President Roosevelt had first used the term "united nations" in 1942 to describe the nations fighting Nazi and Japanese tyranny. During the war, representatives from many countries met several times to form an organization that would promote international peace and cooperation.

In June 1945, representatives from 50 nations signed the United Nation's charter, or founding document. In October, the UN charter went into effect when the governments of the United States, Great Britain, France, and China approved it. These five nations became the permanent members of the governing body of the United Nations, the Security Council.

Membership in such an international organization was a change in U.S. tradition that was supported by most Americans. The horrors of the war had shown that the nation could not hope to stay out of conflicts elsewhere in the world and still have peace and security at home.

CHAPTER 6

A WARM WELCOME HOME, A COLD WAR ABROAD, 1946–1948

AFTER THE JAPANESE SURRENDER, THE vast U.S. military shrank quickly as soldiers, sailors, and airmen returned home and reentered civilian life. In May 1945, the U.S. Army's worldwide strength stood at 8.3 million men. By the end of 1945, half of these men and women were out of uniform, and three years later the army would number less than 600,000, many of them on occupation duty in Germany and Japan.

A massive crowd gathered in New York City's Times Square to celebrate Japan's surrender and the end of the war. *(Library of Congress)*

"Prices soar,
buyers sore."

—New York newspaper headline referring to inflation, 1946

Many Americans worried that the returning G.I.s would have a hard time adjusting to civilian life. Some of the 700,000 wounded during the war did come home having lost a limb or their sight, or they were suffering from other terrible injuries. Many other veterans were mentally and emotionally wounded by their experiences in combat. The vast majority of the young people who had served overseas, however, gladly put away their uniforms, enjoyed a few months of rest, and then got on with their lives.

The G.I.'s path back to civilian life was smoothed by a remarkable piece of legislation: the Readjustment Act of 1944, better known as the G.I. Bill of Rights. The law provided about $14 billion in government funds to help returning servicemen secure education, housing, medical care, and job training for themselves.

The G.I. Bill changed life in America in several ways. First, it helped create a highly educated workforce. Before World War II, relatively few students went on to college after high school, mainly because of the cost. The G.I. Bill paid the cost of college tuition, putting a college degree within the reach of many veterans who would not otherwise have been able to afford it. The G.I. Bill also provided money for living expenses for married G.I.s with families so that they, too, could attend college. By 1946, about half of the country's 2 million college students were veterans.

Second, the G.I. Bill led to a large increase in home ownership. Former G.I.s could borrow money to buy homes at a low rate of interest and were given a long time (usually 30 years) to pay off the loan. In 1940, only about one out of every three U.S. families owned their own home. Thanks to the G.I. Bill, by 1950 that figure had risen to two out of every three families.

Third, the G.I. Bill helped veterans find a place in the postwar economy. At the war's end, there were worries that there would not be enough jobs for the millions of veterans. Some feared a postwar recession like the one that had followed World War I. To help returning G.I.s make ends meet while looking for jobs, the G.I. Bill provided an unemployment benefit of $20 per week for 52 weeks. In fact, most veterans found jobs quickly and were only in the so-called 52/20 Club for a couple of months.

The feared recession did not happen. Instead, the wartime boom carried over into peacetime. Because so many consumer goods had been rationed or were unavailable during the war years, U.S. workers had saved the money they would otherwise have spent on new cars, appliances, and other items. Now that many Americans had more money in the bank than ever before, there was a great demand for consumer goods. As a result, there were plenty of jobs available for veterans.

The G.I. Bill also helped veterans by providing loans for job training, so that returning G.I.s could learn new trades and get better jobs. Veterans could also receive low-interest loans to buy their own businesses.

The return of so many veterans led to a severe shortage of housing. Here, three vets, attending the University of Wisconsin on the G.I. Bill, camp out in a tent to protest the point. *(Library of Congress)*

FUN AT THE DRIVE-IN

The first new cars since 1940 rolled out of auto plants in 1946. With an end to gas and tire rationing, Americans took to the road again in ever-increasing numbers. Now they could go to the movies in the privacy and comfort of their cars. Between 1947 and 1950, about 2,000 drive-in movie theaters opened across the country. The drive-in was usually located in a field with a huge screen at one end. Sound was provided by loudspeakers mounted on posts driven into the ground or smaller speakers that were clipped to car door window frames. Drive-ins also offered snack bars, which served a new food item—pizza. The first pizza parlors opened in the United States in the 1890s, but it was not until after World War II, when G.I.s returned from service in Italy, that pizza became popular.

If the moviegoers skipped the snack bar, they could stop at one of the new drive-in restaurants on the way home and be served in their car by waiters or waitresses, called carhops. In 1948, Richard and Maurice McDonald opened a drive-in (without the carhops) in San Bernardino, California. There were only three items on the menu: hamburgers (15 cents), French fries (10 cents), and milkshakes (25 cents). By the 21st century, there would be about 30,000 McDonald's restaurants in 119 countries.

Although a 1945 poll found that the majority of women defense workers hoped to continue working after the war ended, most would be out of the job as millions of G.I.'s came home. *(Library of Congress)*

On July 4, 1946, the Philippines became an independent nation after nearly a half-century of rule by the United States and three years of Japanese occupation during World War II.

WOMEN RETURN TO THE HOME

While millions of veterans applied for work in the nation's factories and shops, millions of women left the workforce. At the end of the war, more than 20 million women worked outside the home—more than a third of the total workforce. By 1947, about 5 million women had left the workforce entirely, while millions more lost well-paid, full-time factory jobs and had to take lower-paid, less-skilled, part-time work.

After Pearl Harbor, politicians and newspapers told women that it was their patriotic duty to work so that male workers could enter the military. With the war over, women were told it was their patriotic duty to give up their jobs to returning servicemen and return to being full-time wives and mothers.

Some historians believe that three-quarters of the female World War II workforce had hoped to continue working after the war's end. Unfortunately for these women, the pressure to return home was too great. In any case, millions of women would remember the war years as a time when they proved they could do a man's job. Over the next several decades, the experience of women on the World War II home front would help spark the movement for greater opportunities for women in all areas of life.

CIVIL RIGHTS AFTER THE WAR

The wartime years made African Americans more determined to fight prejudice and segregation. African Americans had fought to save much of Europe and Asia from tyranny, but when they came home, some found that they were still denied political and civil rights. Some African-American veterans, for example, would later remember how angry they had been to see German and Italian prisoners of war eating in all-white segregated southern restaurants, while they (black veterans) were turned away because of their race. The National Association for the Advancement of Colored People (NAACP) began to draw attention to the problem through large rallies and public demonstrations.

President Truman was a supporter of civil rights. In 1946, Truman set up the Commission on Civil Rights, which called for fairness in hiring African Americans for employment by the federal government. The commission also demanded an end to the poll tax. This was a special local tax, levied in several southern states, which made it impossible for many African Americans to vote because they were too poor to pay it.

Unfortunately, the Commission on Civil Rights did not have the power to put these ideas into practice. The president's Democratic Party included many white southern politicians who fought efforts to end segregation and guarantee civil rights for African Americans.

President Harry Truman speaks at an NAACP rally in Washington, D.C. *(Library of Congress)*

The NAACP organized legal challenges and protests against racial discrimination, including this 1947 demonstration against school segregation in Houston, Texas. *(Library of Congress)*

Air conditioning, rare before the war, rapidly became a part of American life in the late 1940s. Thirty thousand room air conditioners were sold in 1946; by the early 1950s, more than a million were being produced each year.

United Mine Workers Union (UMW) President John L. Lewis. Lewis was a determined opponent of the Taft-Hartley Act. (*Library of Congress*)

The Truman administration did take one big step forward in civil rights, however, by desegregating the military. Although some military officers still questioned the intelligence and ability of African Americans, their performance in the war had proved that they were excellent soldiers. In July 1948, Truman signed Executive Order 9981, which called for "equality of treatment and opportunity for all persons in the armed services without regard to race, color, religion or national origin." African Americans would now serve alongside whites, and they would have the opportunity to become officers.

LABOR AFTER THE WAR

The number of U.S. workers who were union members doubled between 1940 and 1950. By the end of the decade more than a third of all workers belonged to a union. During the war, the federal government controlled wages and set prices for many goods to keep inflation under control. In 1946, however, the Truman administration ended most of these controls. As a result, prices of goods began to rise. Union workers in many industries went on strike for higher pay.

The most serious strike of the postwar years began later that year when United Mine Workers (UMW) leader John L. Lewis led many of the nation's coal miners off the job once again. Several railroad unions then threatened to go on strike in support of the miners. If railroad workers joined the strike, a major part of the country's transportation network would be shut down.

In May, President Truman threatened to use the federal government to take control of the strikebound coal mines. He also threatened to draft railroad workers into the U.S. Army if they went out on strike. The UMW then agreed to a deal with the mine owners, and the trains kept rolling.

Despite his actions in the 1946 strike, Truman was a strong supporter of organized labor. That year's

RALPH BUNCHE, PEACEMAKER

After World War II many of the European Jews who had survived Nazi concentration camps wanted to move to Palestine—the ancient homeland of the Jewish people. Modern-day Palestine, however, had a large Arab population, many of whom did not want more Jews as their neighbors. Britain, which ruled Palestine under the authority of the United Nations, had tried to keep the peace between Jews and Arabs, but on May 15, 1948, British forces left Palestine. Jewish leaders proclaimed a new nation—the state of Israel. Fighting between Arabs and Jews broke out immediately. A UN

Ralph Bunche won the Nobel Peace Prize in 1951. *(Library of Congress)*

representative, Folke Bemadotte of Sweden, negotiated a truce (an end to the fighting), but it fell apart after he was killed. The difficult job of making peace between Jews and Arabs then went to Ralph Bunche, an African-American educator working for the United Nations. Bunche managed to bring both sides to the peace table in May 1949. For his brilliant diplomacy, the following year Bunche received the Nobel Peach Prize, one of the highest international honors. Bunche undertook further peacemaking missions for the United Nations until his retirement in 1965.

elections, however, gave the Republican Party a majority in both houses of Congress. Many Republican politicians were eager to limit the power of the unions.

In 1947, Senator Robert Taft and Representative Fred Hartley introduced a bill that would become known as the Taft-Hartley Act. The act was designed to overturn so-called closed-shop laws in some states. (Closed shops banned the hiring of nonunion workers.) The law also required unions to report their finances to the government and gave companies the right to sue unions for the loss of business due to strikes. The most controversial part of the proposed act called for a cooling-off period of 60 days before any strike. The law also gave the president the power to stop strikes that threatened the national economy. Truman vetoed the bill, but Congress overrode the veto, and the Taft-Hartley Act became law in June 1947.

Although the Taft-Hartley Act limited what unions could do, the law did not prove to be a major setback for organized labor. Union membership continued to grow, as would the political power of the biggest unions,

On December 31, 1946, the Flamingo Hotel and Casino opened in Las Vegas, Nevada, beginning Las Vegas's transformation from a sleepy desert town into America's gambling-and-entertainment capital.

Harry Truman made the first televised speech by a president on October 5, 1947. He appealed to Americans to save food so that aid shipments to war-ravaged Europe and Asia could be increased.

In 1946, the Roman Catholic Church canonized Mother Frances Xavier Cabrini as the first American saint. Cabrini, who was born in Italy in 1850 and became a U.S. citizen in 1909, founded the Missionary Sisters of the Sacred Heart religious order and became known as the "the saint of the immigrants."

especially the American Federation of Labor and Congress of Industrial Organizations (AFL/CIO).

THE COLD WAR BEGINS

In March 1946, Winston Churchill, former wartime leader of Great Britain, traveled to Fulton, Missouri, to give a speech at Westminster College. In his address, he noted that "an iron curtain has descended across Europe." Churchill's words summed up the growing fear that despite the Allied victory, communist domination had replaced Nazi tyranny in much of Central and Eastern Europe.

The Soviets had promised to hold free, democratic elections in Poland, Hungary, Czechoslovakia, Romania, and the other Eastern European nations they had occupied at the end of the war. Instead, the Soviets crushed all noncommunist political parties and installed communist governments and leaders who were easily controlled from Moscow. In addition, the Soviets supported communist movements in the rest of Europe, including France, Italy, and Greece. Many Americans now believed that the Soviet Union's expansion in Europe and the spread of communist governments threatened the national security of the United States.

Having just fought a world war, few Americans wanted to get into a conflict with the Soviet Union. The Truman Administration tried to find ways to stop the spread of communism without fighting the Soviets directly. This policy became known as containment.

One way to halt the spread of communism was to supply money, weapons, and other help to nations fighting communist-supported rebels. In Greece, for example, the government was struggling against communist guerrillas who were receiving aid from neighboring communist countries.

In February 1947, President Truman asked Congress for $400 million worth of military and other aid for

Greece and Turkey. In doing so, Truman made it clear that the United States was willing to support countries around the world in their struggles against communism. This policy became known as the Truman Doctrine.

Later in 1947, concern over the spread of communism led Congress to pass a far-reaching law known as the National Security Act. The act created a new organization, the Central Intelligence Agency (CIA), to gather and distribute secret information about possible threats to the nation's security from other nations. (Before the establishment of the CIA, such activities were the responsibility of several agencies.) Although intelligence gathering was the CIA's main mission, within a few years the CIA began secret operations against foreign governments that were thought to be unfriendly to the United States.

The National Security Act also created the National Security Council, a committee of national security and foreign policy specialists, high-ranking politicians, and military officers who regularly advised the president on matters of national security.

Not everyone was happy with these developments. Many liberals believed that it was better to try to negotiate with the Soviets rather than challenging them. Some Americans also feared that the new laws gave the military too much power and allowed the military and the CIA to operate in secrecy, without control from Congress and without the knowledge of the public. On the other hand, some people felt that the United States was not acting forcefully enough to stop the spread of communism.

THE MARSHALL PLAN

The cold war was also a war of ideas. The United States and its allies needed to convince the people of western Europe and of the rest of the world that democracy offered a better way of life than communism.

NEW RECORDS

The recorded music industry bounced back from its wartime slump after the introduction of two new kinds of records. The first was the LP, or long-playing record, developed by Columbia Records, which was first introduced in 1948.

Before the LP, the most common type of record was the 10-inch 78, so-called because it revolved 78 times a minute on a record player. The 78, however, could hold only about three minutes of music on each side. The 10- or 12-inch LP, which revolved 33½ times per minute, could hold 20 to 30 minutes of music.

The LP was also made of vinyl (a type of plastic) instead of shellac, which improved the sound and made it more durable than the 78. In 1949, RCA introduced the 7-inch 45, which soon replaced the 78 as the record of choice for popular songs.

Music lovers also enjoyed a new radio technology. Frequency Modulation (FM) offered much better sound than the older Amplitude Modulation (AM) standard. The first modern FM station, W47MV in Nashville, Tennessee, began broadcasting in 1945.

"Let us not be deceived. We are today in the midst of a cold war. Our enemies are to be found abroad and at home."

—Government adviser Bernard Baruch in a speech on April 16, 1947

"Berlin rebuilds with the help of the Marshall Plan," reads this poster, which also bears the logo of the European Recovery Program—the Marshall Plan's official name. *(Library of Congress)*

World War II had left Europe shattered. The economies of France, Italy, and other nations were in ruins. Years after the fighting ended, millions of Europeans were still jobless, hungry, and homeless. Many Americans believed that if the United States did not help put Europe back on its feet, communist influence would grow there.

One American who was convinced that Europe needed U.S. help was George C. Marshall, the U.S. Army's Chief of Staff in World War II and now secretary of State. In a June 1947 speech at Harvard University, Marshall proposed a major U.S. aid program for Europe. Congress approved the program, which quickly became known as the Marshall Plan.

Over the next four years the United States sent more than $23 billion worth of aid to 16 European countries—delivering food, medical supplies, seeds, fertilizer, factory machinery, tools, and many other goods. The United States also offered aid to the Soviet Union and the communist countries of Eastern Europe, but under pressure from Soviet dictator Joseph Stalin, all refused to be part of the program.

The Marshall Plan was a huge success. By the end of the decade, the economies of Western Europe were prospering. The plan benefited the U.S. economy, too. Now that western Europe had recovered from the war, Europeans now had the money to buy U.S. goods. The result created jobs in the United States and kept the postwar economy booming.

THE BERLIN AIRLIFT

The first big clash of the cold war in Europe came in Germany. At the end of World War II, the United States, Britain, France, and the Soviet Union each occupied a section or zone of Germany. The plan was to reunite Germany eventually. In 1948, the three western allies combined their occupation zones into a new coun-

C-47 transport planes unload their cargoes under floodlights at Berlin's Tempelhof Airport in July 1948. All in all, the planes brought 2.3 million tons of supplies into the city. *(Library of Congress)*

try—the Federal Republic of Germany, or West Germany. In protest, the Soviets cut off access to Berlin, Germany's largest city, in June 1948. Berlin was divided into an Allied-ruled zone (West Berlin) and a Soviet-ruled zone (East Berlin). However, the city itself was located deep inside the eastern, Soviet-occupied part of Germany. Food, fuel, and other supplies coming into the city by road, water, or railroad had to pass through Soviet-occupied territory. Now that the Soviets refused to allow goods to reach West Berlin, its citizens faced hardship and perhaps even starvation.

Some advisers urged President Truman to use military force to reopen the roads to Berlin. Instead the president and British leaders decided to supply West Berlin by air. Flying from West Germany, U.S. and British military pilots flew round-the-clock missions to bring food, coal, medicine, and other vital materials into Berlin.

The Berlin Airlift, as it was called, lasted almost a year. Finally, in May 1949, Stalin backed down and reopened the roads into West Berlin. The airlift was a major victory for the United States and its allies.

"We will continue to do our part to help other countries to help themselves."

— President Truman,
July 5, 1947

The annual Antoinette Perry Awards (a.k.a. the Tonies) for excellence in the theater were awarded for the first time on April 7, 1947. Playwright Arthur Miller won Best Author for *All My Sons.*

Seven of the so-called Hollywood Ten are shown here during their 1947 trial for contempt of Congress. *(Library of Congress)*

THE COLD WAR AT HOME

The chill of the cold war also entered the daily lives of Americans in the postwar years. While the United States tried to halt the spread of communism overseas, many people became convinced that the nation also faced a threat at home from Americans spying for the Soviet Union.

There was some truth to this fear. There were a small number of Americans, some of them in important government positions, secretly working for the Soviets. However, the extent of Soviet spying in the United States would not be known until many years later.

At the time, many politicians from both parties pressured President Truman to make sure there were no Communist Party members working for the government. In 1947, Truman ordered all federal workers to swear an oath of loyalty to the U.S. government.

A special congressional committee, the House Un-American Activities Committee (HUAC), also investigated communist influence, not only in the government but

FIRST STEPS TOWARD SPACE

At the end of the war the United States brought German scientist Wernher von Braun and many of his colleagues to Fort Bliss, Texas. Braun had developed the V-2 rocket for the German military, and now he put his experience to work on the new U.S. rocket program. Working in secret in White Sands, New Mexico, the German scientists and their U.S. Army counterparts assembled rockets from captured German parts. The first successful launch took place on April 16, 1946. The U.S. Army was immediately interested in rockets for military purposes, but the work also led to further developments in rocket science.

White Sands also marked the start of the U.S. space program, which would take humans to the moon just 23 years later. At about the same time, the U.S. Air Force was experimenting with piloted, rocket-powered aircraft. On October 14, 1947, Captain Chuck Yeager strapped himself into the Bell X-I rocket plane. Carried into the air in the belly of a B-29 bomber, the X-I was released at 20,000 feet. The rocket engine powered the X-1 to a speed of more than 700 miles per hour—faster than the speed of sound. Yeager returned to earth as the first human to have broken the sound barrier in level flight.

The Bell X-1 was the first aircraft to fly faster than the speed of sound in level flight. Pilot Chuck Yeager named the rocket-powered plane after his wife, Glennis Dickhouse Yeager. *(Library of Congress)*

---

also in organized labor, in colleges and universities, and even in the movie industry.

Some of the people investigated by the HUAC refused to cooperate because they believed the committee's activities were unconstitutional. In 1947, a group of Hollywood screenwriters refused to "name names" to HUAC; that is, identify communists and people suspected of being Communist Party members. For this refusal, in 1948, a federal court convicted the so-called Hollywood Ten of contempt of Congress in 1948 and sentenced them to prison terms of up to a year. When the screenwriters were released from prison, they found themselves blacklisted, meaning that the movie studios refused to hire them.

The committee's most famous investigation involved Alger Hiss, a high-ranking diplomat in the State Department. In 1948, a magazine editor and former Communist Party member named Whittaker

Dad reads the evening paper and the kids watch TV. Beneath such peaceful scenes lurked a growing anxiety about communism and the cold war, which helped encourage HUAC. *(Library of Congress)*

"Ninety-nine percent of us are well aware of what's going on."

—Screen Actors Guild president Ronald Reagan, speaking to HUAC about the influence of Communist Party members in Hollywood

Thanks to an $8.5 million donation from financier John D. Rockefeller, the United Nations bought land for a permanent home along the East River in New York City. The cornerstone of the headquarters building was laid on October 1949.

Chambers accused Hiss of working for the Soviet Union from the late 1930s on. Hiss denied the charge and sued Chambers. After two trials, in 1949 and 1950, a federal jury found Hiss guilty of perjury (lying or withholding information while under oath) and sentenced him to five years in prison. Released after three years, for the rest of his life Hiss claimed that he was innocent. In the 1990s, however, new evidence came to light that made a strong case that Hiss had indeed been a Soviet spy.

Some Americans found the loyalty oath and the HUAC investigations troubling. Freedom of speech and the right to hold political opinions, even if they are unpopular, are among the foundations of U.S. democracy. Now the government seemed to be weakening that foundation in the ongoing hunt for Communist Party members. Other Americans believed that anticommunist activities were justified because of the threat that the Soviet Union posed to the peace and security of the United States and to the free, noncommunist world.

CHAPTER 7

BRIGHTER DAYS AHEAD, 1948–1950

AS THE PRESIDENTIAL ELECTION YEAR of 1948 began, most Americans believed there would be a new president in the White House in 1949. President Truman announced that he would run for a second term, but he was very unpopular, even in his own Democratic Party. Truman was so unpromising a candidate that two different groups of Democrats broke away from the party and nominated their own presidential hopefuls.

The first was the States Rights Party, known as the Dixiecrats. This group included conservative white southerners who opposed Truman's support for civil rights for African Americans. The Dixiecrats nominated South Carolina governor Strom Thurmond for president.

Thomas Dewey was so heavily favored to win the election of 1948 that some newspapers ran headlines proclaiming "Dewey Defeats Truman" after the polls closed. *(Library of Congress)*

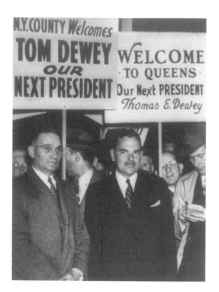

Republicans greet Thomas Dewey on a campaign tour of New York City. Dewey served as governor of the state from 1943 until 1955. *(Library of Congress)*

"The most popular, and probably the best, service that Truman could render to his party now is to step aside."

—Newspaper editorial, 1948

The second group, made up primarily of liberal Democrats in the northern states, formed the Progressive Party. The Progressives were opposed the use of the loyalty oath and wanted to improve relations with the Soviet Union. The Progressives' candidate was Henry Wallace, who had served as vice president under Franklin Roosevelt and was now secretary of agriculture.

The presence of two Democratic third-party candidates on the ballot meant that Truman would lose the votes of many Democrats who would normally vote for the party's nominee. In addition, the president had to meet a strong challenge from the Republicans, who again nominated New York governor Thomas Dewey. Dewey chose California governor Earl Warren as his vice-presidential running mate.

Despite polls that confidently predicted his defeat, Truman came out fighting. He toured the country by train, making fiery speeches at small towns along the way. He focused on what he called the "do-nothing" Republican majority in Congress, who were blocking the passage of laws the country needed. Truman's message and his plain-speaking, no-nonsense style won over many people. In contrast, Governor Dewey was an uninspiring speaker.

When the country went to the polls, the result was a huge upset. Truman easily beat Dewey by more than 2 million votes. Wallace got about 1.2 million votes, as did Thurmond. Although Thurmond lost, the Dixiecrats won in the electoral college in the states of Louisiana, Mississippi, Alabama, and South Carolina and tied with Truman in Tennessee. Thurmond's strong showing in the South showed the deep divisions in the country over civil rights.

Besides keeping the White House, Democratic Party candidates gained majorities in the Senate and the House of Representatives, ending the Republican majority after just two years. Democrats also gained the governorship of several states.

After the election Truman announced his support for a sweeping program that he called the Fair Deal. It included civil rights laws, more federal money for education and housing, an expansion of the Social Security system, and an end to the Taft-Hartley Act. Truman soon found that the new Democratic majority could be just as difficult as the Republicans. In the end, Congress passed only one major Fair Deal law. This was the National Housing Act of 1949, which provided money for the construction of more than 800,000 homes for poorer Americans.

HOLDING THE LINE OVERSEAS

The Soviet threat in Europe led some Western European and U.S. leaders to consider a military partnership. They knew that France, Britain, and other European nations would not be able to withstand a Soviet invasion. But if the nations of Western Europe presented a united front, backed by the military might of the United States, they might discourage the Soviets from trying to spread communist rule to more countries in Europe.

In 1948, France, Belgium, Britain, Luxembourg, and the Netherlands formed a military alliance. In 1949, U.S. and European representatives met to discuss bringing the United States into this partnership. The result was the North Atlantic Treaty Organization (NATO), which included the nations listed above as well as the United States, Canada, and Iceland, which had become independent of Denmark in June 1944.

The NATO treaty had to be approved by the Senate, and there was much debate about it. World War II and the start of the cold war had done away with isolationism. Still, joining an international military alliance in peacetime was a big change in U.S. tradition. In any case, the Senate ratified the NATO treaty in July 1949, and Congress agreed to provide more than $1 billion in weapons and other military aid to the NATO nations.

The Stuart family of Arkansas, shown here, was the first African-American family to receive a loan under the Housing Act of 1949. *(Library of Congress)*

Inventor Edwin Land introduced the Polaroid camera in 1948. Ushering in the age of "instant" photography, it took just one minute to develop a snapshot.

"Every segment of our population and every individual has a right to expect from his government a fair deal."

—President Harry Truman, January 1949

President Harry Truman displays a copy of the North Atlantic Treaty Organization (NATO) Charter, signed by the United States and 11 other countries in Washington, D.C., in April 1949. *(Library of Congress)*

"An armed attack against one or more [of the member nations] in Europe or North America shall be considered an attack upon them all."

—From the NATO Charter, 1949

The cold war got a lot colder just a month later, when U.S. planes flying high above the northern Pacific found evidence of radiation in the air. This data made it clear that the Soviet Union had successfully tested an atomic bomb. For four years the United States had been the only nation to possess atomic weapons. No one had expected the Soviets to build an atomic bomb so quickly. (It would later become known that the Soviets received help from U.S. spies.)

Now Americans had to worry about the possibility of a nuclear war between the United States and the Soviet Union. The constant threat of a nuclear war would be part of Americans' daily lives for decades to come.

Events in Asia added to Americans' worries as the 1940s ended. At the end of World War II, civil war swept China as Communist forces led by Mao Zedong battled the Nationalist armies of Chiang Kai-shek. At the end of 1949, Mao forced the Nationalist government to flee to the offshore island of Taiwan (then called Formosa) and proclaimed that the People's Republic of China was the only true government of China. The world's most populous nation was now Communist. Many Americans feared that Red China (as it was often called) and the Soviet Union together would dominate the smaller nations of the world.

POSTWAR PROSPERITY AND THE BABY BOOM

Americans in the late 1940s worried about events overseas, but many found much to be happy about at home. By 1948, inflation was mostly under control and jobs continued to be plentiful. The nation's industries poured out consumer goods in greater numbers and variety than at any time since the 1920s, and lots of Americans had the money to buy them. It was the start of a period of postwar prosperity that would last until the mid-1970s.

One the most important developments of the postwar years was a big increase in the number of babies born, as G.I.s returned home to their wives or married and started families. This rise in the number of births was called the baby boom. More than 75 million Americans were born between 1946 and 1964, when the boom ended, and most of these people were born between 1946 and 1957. By the year 2000, baby boomers made up between a quarter and a third of the U.S. population.

Many young postwar families chose to live in suburbs—communities close to, but separate from major cities. Together with the baby boom, the rise of suburbia would change the face of U.S. society.

There were a number of reasons for the big growth of suburbs after World War II. First of all, there was a shortage of housing in the cities during and after the war. Second, thanks to the G.I. Bill, many veterans could afford to buy a house of their own rather than rent a city apartment. Third, affordable cars and better roads made it possible for workers to live a distance from their jobs in the cities.

The most famous suburb of the time was Levittown, outside of New York City. In 1946, real estate developer William Levitt saw an opportunity in the postwar housing shortage. He decided to buy up farmland on Long Island and build thousands of houses, all constructed

DR. SPOCK

During the baby boom millions of parents turned to a single book for advice on how to raise their offspring: *The Common Sense Book of Baby and Child Care.* Pocket Books published the book in 1946—just in time for the baby boom—and it originally sold for 25 cents. It eventually sold more than 50 million copies, which at the time made it the second bestselling book (besides the Bible) in history.

The author was pediatrician Benjamin Spock, and his advice to parents marked a break with the past. Spock told parents to trust their instincts when it came to child raising and urged them to be friends with their children. One famous line from the book declared, "There is no such thing as a bad boy." Spock's book had a huge influence on the generations born after World War II. Although many associate his theories with 1950s child rearing, millions of copies of the book were sold prior to 1950. Spock later became a controversial figure when he spoke out against the Vietnam War in the 1960s.

An aerial view shows the layout of Levittown, Pennsylvania, located midway between Philadelphia, Pennsylvania, and Trenton, New Jersey, in the early 1950s. *(Library of Congress)*

With a horizontal roof, carport, and sliding glass doors opening to the outdoors, this suburban home on Long Island exhibits the features typical of postwar style. *(Library of Congress)*

"Me? Naw—I'm prewar."

"Me? Naw—I'm prewar," proclaims a youngster in this 1948 cartoon by Bill Mauldin— a comment on the increase in the U.S. birthrate during and after World War II. *(Library of Congress)*

according to standard plans. Each house came complete with a stove, a refrigerator, and other appliances and sold for $8,000.

When the first Levittown homes went on sale in 1947, hundreds of buyers, most of them veterans, camped out all night to be first in line at the sales office. By 1951, Levittown grew to include more than 17,000 homes. Levitt went on to build more Levittowns in other states, and developers across the country rushed to build similar communities.

Not everyone liked the new suburbs. Some Americans wondered why people would want to live in communities in which every house looked much like every other house. And while schools sprang up in the suburbs to educate the baby boomers, the suburbs lacked the cultural riches of cities, such as museums, art galleries, and concert halls. Other critics of the suburbs believed that they lacked the sense of community and solidarity found in city neighborhoods, where people lived closer together and had more involvement in each other's daily lives. Most suburban residents, however, enjoyed their new lifestyle. Suburbanites soon added personal touches to their mass-produced houses. Suburban homes also offered backyards to relax in.

Cars were the key to life in the suburb. Most houses had a garage or carport sheltering one or more cars. Cars allowed fathers to get to work at the office or the factory and allowed mothers to shop at the supermarket (another convenient feature of suburban life) and bring children to Little League games, Boy Scout and Girl Scout meetings, and other after-school activities.

The rising demand for cars led to good times for the nation's automobile industry. In 1949, some 6 million cars rolled off the assembly lines at Ford, General Motors, Chrysler, and other companies, more than during any previous year. Related industries, such as steel, rubber, and glass, benefited from the demand for cars, too.

The growing rate of car ownership, however, was not without problems. All the new cars on the road needed gasoline, which is made from oil. In the 1940s, the United States still got most of its oil from sources within its own borders. As demand for oil grew, however, the United States had to buy more oil from overseas, especially from Middle Eastern countries such as Iran and Saudi Arabia.

THE TELEVISION REVOLUTION

At the start of the 1940s, Americans got their news and entertainment from the radio and the movies. By the end of the decade, both radio and the movies faced stiff competition from a new technology—television, or as it would soon be known, TV.

Several inventors developed the technology behind television in the first decades of the 20th century. By the 1930s, a number of countries were experimenting with television broadcasts. In 1939, for example, the Radio Corporation of America (RCA) broadcast President Roosevelt speaking at the opening ceremony of the New York World's Fair. At that time there were only a few hundred televisions in the entire country.

The government stopped television production in 1942 because their electronic components were needed for the war effort. The ban was lifted in 1946, and by the end of that year Americans had bought about 40,000 televisions, most of them built with a five-inch, black-and-white screen housed in a big, boxy wooden cabinet.

Television was not an overnight success, mostly because early sets were expensive. A 1946 RCA set cost $350, more than a month's salary for the average U.S. worker. As a result, most television sets were found mainly in bars and other public places rather than in homes. Baseball games and boxing matches were the

FLYING SAUCERS

On June 24, 1947, pilot Kenneth Arnold reported seeing strange "crescent-shaped" objects flying close to his plane over Mount Rainier in Washington State. Soon people all over the country claimed to have seen similar flying saucers in the sky. Some thought they were experimental aircraft from a secret government project; others believed aliens from outer space piloted them. A month after the Mount Rainier sightings, things got stranger when news reports circulated that people in Roswell, New Mexico, had seen the bodies of strange creatures and a crashed spacecraft.

There was so much excitement over flying saucers that the U.S. Air Force set up Project Sign, which investigated 244 sightings of Unidentified Flying Objects (UFOs). In 1949, the project's report stated that there was no evidence that the objects came from outer space.

Nevertheless, speculating about UFOs and aliens has been a popular activity ever since. (As for the Roswell incident, in the 1990s the U.S. Air Force reported that what appeared to be alien bodies were actually crash test dummies, which had been dropped by parachute in an experiment.)

MR. TELEVISION

No one did more to make the television the center of the U.S. living room than comedian Milton Berle. Like several early television stars, Berle got his start in vaudeville, which included live shows featuring a mix of comedians, singers, magicians, and novelty acts such as performing animals. When the popularity of movies ended the heydey of vaudeville in the 1930s, Berle moved on to radio. Then, in 1948, he landed on television as host of the NBC network's *Texaco Star Theater*.

Berle did it all—he told jokes, did impressions, and danced, usually while

sporting outrageous costumes. He quickly became television's most popular entertainer, earning $6,500 per week (a huge salary at the time) and winning the nicknames Uncle Miltie and Mr. Television. It was said that many families bought their first televisions just so they could watch Berle's show. He continued to host *Texaco Star Theater* until 1955. In 1984, he was one of the first seven people elected to the Television Academy Hall of Fame.

Milton Berle strikes a characteristically wacky pose in this publicity photo. *(Library of Congress)*

---

most popular shows. Also, at this time television signals could only be broadcast to cover relatively short distances, usually in and around big cities. (By contrast, there were 40 million radios in America in the mid-1940s, and four radio networks broadcasting nationwide.)

Television started to take off in 1948 as prices dropped, when three-inch sets sold for as low as $100. At the same time, television stations increased their broadcast range by sending signals through cables or using new microwave technology. In January 1949, cable linked the East Coast with the Midwest, though the first coast-to-coast broadcast would not take place until 1951.

By late 1949, there were 2 million televisions in the United States; a year later there were 8 million. By the 1960s, 98 percent of U.S. homes had at least one set. No other technology—including the telephone, the car, and radio—became such a big part of U.S. life in such a short time. For millions of U.S. families, gathering around the television after dinner soon became a daily ritual.

Early television programming was patterned on radio programming. The daytime hours brought a mix of news (for example, *Meet the Press,* which began

"Draw your family circle closer with a Magnavox television."

—Television advertisement, 1949

broadcasting in November 1947, children's shows (such as *Puppet Time Theater*, better known as *The Howdy Doody Show*, which also began in late 1947), and the dramas popularly known as soap operas.

Movies remained popular, but by the late 1940s, ticket sales had fallen well below what they had been a few years earlier. More and more Americans preferred the convenience of staying in their living rooms and watching television instead of going out to the movies. Television also had the advantage of being free to the viewer. Television programming was paid for by the companies who sponsored shows, and by the companies who paid networks to broadcast their commercials, which interrupted programs to sell products to the viewers.

POSTWAR ART AND LITERATURE

Despite the competition from television, U.S. theater enjoyed a golden era in the late 1940s. Following the success of *Oklahoma!* in 1943, a series of brilliant musicals opened on Broadway, including *Annie Get Your Gun*, *Carousel*, *Brigadoon*, *Kiss Me Kate*, and *South Pacific*, which was based on author James Michener's popular book of short stories set during the Pacific campaigns of World War II.

Two powerful playwrights also hit the scene. Tennessee Williams's *The Glass Menagerie* (1945) and *A Streetcar Named Desire* (1947) masterfully explored human relationships. *Streetcar* also made a star out of a struggling young actor named Marlon Brando. Arthur Miller's *Death of a Salesman* (1949) examined the dark side of the struggle for success in business.

Three young novelists, all of them veterans, published bestselling novels of U.S. Army life: Norman Mailer *(The Naked and the Dead)*, Irwin Shaw *(The Young Lions)*, and James Jones *(From Here to Eternity)*. One of the outstanding nonfiction books of the time was John Hersey's *Hiroshima*, adapted from his article in *The New*

Hosted by Buffalo Bob Smith and his sidekick, a 27-inch-long marionette, *The Howdy Doody Show*'s 2,343 episodes aired between 1947 and 1960. *(Library of Congress)*

"It's Howdy Doody time
It's Howdy Doody time
Bob Smith and Howdy too
Say Howdy-Doo to you."

—*Puppet Time Theater* theme song

Marlon Brando shot to fame in 1948 with his portrayal of Stanley Kowalski in the Broadway production of Tennessee Williams's *A Streetcar Named Desire.* *(Library of Congress)*

Norman Mailer's first novel, *The Naked and the Dead,* was published in 1948. The book was based on his own experiences as a G.I. in the Pacific. *(Library of Congress)*

Yorker magazine, which told the story of the first atomic bombing and its aftermath.

While big bands and smooth-sounding singers continued to dominate popular music, classical music enjoyed a wide audience, too. Millions of Americans listened to the radio broadcasts of the NBC Symphony Orchestra, conducted by Arturo Toscanini, who had escaped to the United States from Fascist Italy. Another outstanding conductor was Leonard Bernstein, who was also a brilliant composer and music educator. Composer Aaron Copland wrote music with uniquely U.S. themes, such as *Fanfare for the Common Man, A Lincoln Portrait,* and the score for dancer Martha Graham's 1944 ballet *Appalachian Spring.*

In the visual arts, the big news in the late 1940s was a new style of painting called abstract expressionism. The New York–based abstract expressionists, also known as action painters, slathered big canvases with wild splashes and streaks of paint. The leading abstract expressionist painter was Jackson Pollock. (Some critics dubbed him Jack the Dripper, from his painting style). Others included Robert Motherwell and the Dutch-born Willem de Kooning.

POSTWAR SPORTS

Baseball was the most popular spectator sport in the 1940s. After the end of the war, the professional players swapped their military uniforms for their team jerseys and took to the field again. The Detroit Tigers beat the Chicago Cubs in the first postwar world series (1945), but the American League's New York Yankees won the Fall Classic in 1947, 1949, and 1950, thanks to prewar stars, such as Joe DiMaggio, and a new generation that included Yogi Berra and Phil Rizzuto.

Boxing had many fans, too, and the greatest boxer of the time was undoubtedly Joe Louis, who had a 12-year run as heavyweight champion of the world

(1937–1949), interrupted by four years of military service in World War II. Ezzard Charles defeated Jersey Joe Walcott to take the title in 1949.

The biggest sports story of the 1940s, however, was one whose importance went far beyond the playing field. Professional baseball had been segregated since the 1880s. Only white players could play in the major leagues; African-American players were restricted to their own Negro Leagues.

In 1945, Branch Rickey, owner of the National League's Brooklyn Dodgers, decided to hire an African-American player to challenge baseball's unspoken policy of segregation, known as the color bar. Rickey settled on Jackie Robinson, shortstop for the Kansas City Monarchs, one of the greatest Negro League teams.

Robinson's batting average was close to .300 and he was famous for his base running, but his playing skills were not the only factors that Rickey took into consideration. Rickey decided that Robinson had the cool courage to tough out the abuse he would receive as the first African-American player in the majors. Robinson had served as an army officer in the war. During that time he was arrested for refusing to move to the back of a bus—where black people were ordered to sit—while serving at a training camp in Texas.

After a season with one of the Dodger farm teams, the Montreal Royals, Robinson started as the first baseman for the Dodgers on April 15, 1947. Despite booing from some Dodger fans and abuse from opposing teams, Robinson always kept his cool. Jackie Robinson went on to help lead the Dodgers to 10 pennants and a 1955 World Series victory.

Jackie Robinson's shattering of baseball's color bar was not just a victory for African Americans. It showed the world that the ideals of freedom and democracy that the United States had fought for overseas in World War II were alive at home as Americans headed into a new decade of promise.

FASHION'S NEW LOOK

During the war years, women's fashions were relatively plain and simple because fabric was rationed for the war effort. With peace came an explosion of creativity in fashion that became known as the New Look. French designer Christian Dior inspired the New Look. His original creations were expensive, but inexpensive U.S. copies soon flooded department stores. The New Look featured long skirts, tight waists, and coordinated accessories, which included hats and shoes, and lots and lots of fabric.

Jackie Robinson once said, "The right of every American to first-class citizenship is the most important issue of our time."
(Private Collection)

GLOSSARY

aircraft carrier   A naval ship built to carry, launch, and land warplanes on its deck.

Allies   The nations united to fight the Axis nations in World War II, including the United States, Great Britain, and the Soviet Union.

Axis   The nations of Germany, Italy, and Japan in World War II.

blacklist   To place a person on a list of people to be denied work or other opportunities because of their political beliefs.

casualties   People killed, wounded, captured, and missing in wartime.

census   The federal government's survey of the nation's population, carried out once every 10 years.

chief of staff   The highest-ranking officer in each of the armed services.

civil rights   The rights guaranteed to Americans in the Constitution, including the right to vote, to a fair trial, and to serve on juries.

codebreakers   Specialists who decipher the enemy's coded communications.

communism   A system of government in which the state controls production and all property is held in common. It calls for an end to private property.

convoy   A group of cargo carriers traveling as a unit. In World War II, cargo ships that were protected from attack by destroyers and other warships.

depression   A period of widespread unemployment and a far-reaching economic slowdown.

destroyer   A small, fast warship designed to fight submarines.

dictator   A leader who rules a country with absolute power.

enlisted men and women   Military personnel who are not officers or NCOs.

executive order   An order based on the authority of the president.

fascism   A system of government based on the belief that the nation or a particular ethnic group is more important than individuals.

G.I. (government issue)   World War II serviceman, so called because all his clothing and other gear was provided by the government.

incumbent   A politician running for re-election to a particular office.

inflation   A sharp increase in the prices of goods and services.

internment   The relocation and detainment of Japanese Americans from the West Coast during World War II.

isolationism   The belief that the United States should not get involved in the affairs of other nations.

Issei   Japanese Americans who are not born in the United States and are not citizens.

K.P. (kitchen police)   Enlisted men who served in the kitchens and mess halls during World War II.

labor union   A group of workers in a particular industry who join together to pressure and persuade employers to give workers a fair wage and better working conditions.

landing craft   Boats built to carry soldiers and vehicles from ships offshore to the beaches.

musical   A play that includes many songs.

Nazi Germany   Germany from the years 1933 to 1945, when the country was ruled by Adolf Hitler and his Nazi Party. Nazi was an abbreviation for National Socialist German Workers' Party.

neutrality   The state of having a position neither for nor against another position. It often refers to a nation that refuses to take sides in a war.

Nissei   Japanese Americans who are born in the United States and are thus U.S. citizens.

Noncommissioned officer (NCO)   Military personnel ranking above enlisted men and below officers.

pacifist   A person who opposes war for any reason.

paratroopers   Soldiers who enter a combat area by parachute after being dropped from airplanes.

perjury   The crime of lying to a jury during a trial.

radiation   A form of energy released in a nuclear reaction.

recession   A period of decreased economic activity and unemployment.

segregation   The system of separate facilities for whites and African Americans in much of the South, which lasted from the 1890s to the 1960s.

veto   The power of the president to prevent bills passed by Congress from becoming law. If the president opposes a bill passed by Congress, he or she can try to stop it from becoming law by refusing to sign it. Congress can override this veto with a two-thirds majority vote.

FURTHER READING

BOOKS

Aaseng, Nathan, and Roy O. Hawthorne. *Navajo Code Talkers*. New York: Walker & Co., 2002.

———. *Band of Brothers*. New York: Simon & Schuster, 2001.

Ambrose, Stephen E. *The Good Fight: How World War II Was Won*. New York: Atheneum, 2001.

———. *Citizen Soldiers*. New York: Simon & Schuster, 1998.

———. *The Wild Blue*. New York: Simon & Schuster, 2001.

America in the '40s: A Sentimental Journey. Pleasantville, N.Y.: Reader's Digest, 1998.

Blum, John Morton. *V Was for Victory: Politics and American Culture During World War II*. New York: Harvest/HBJ, 1977.

Boyer, Paul S. *By the Bomb's Early Light: American Thought and Culture at the Dawn of the Atomic Age*. Chapel Hill: University of North Carolina Press, 1994.

Bradley, James. *Flags of Our Fathers*. New York: Bantam, 2000.

Colman, Penny. *Rosie the Riveter: Women Working on the Home Front in World War II*. New York: Crown Books for Young Readers, 1998.

Feinstein, Stephen. *The 1940s: From World War II to Jackie Robinson*. Berkeley Heights, N.J.: Enslow Publishers, 2000.

Freedman, Russell. *Eleanor Roosevelt: A Life of Discovery*. New York: Clarion Books, 1993.

———. *Franklin Delano Roosevelt*. New York: Clarion Books, 1992.

Gonzales, Doreen. *The Manhattan Project and the Atomic Bomb in American History*. Berkeley Heights, N.J.: Enslow Publishers, 2000.

Hakim, Joy. *All the People 1945–1999 (History of US, Book 10)*. New York: Oxford University Press, 1999.

Hersey, John. *Hiroshima*. New York: Vintage, 1989.

Hill, Prescott. *Our Century: 1940–1950*. Milwaukee, Wisc.: Gareth Stevens Publishing, 1993.

Hoopes, Roy. *Americans Remember the Home Front: An Oral Narrative of the World War II Years in America*. Madison: University of Wisconsin Press, 1985.

Houston, James D., and Jeanne Houston. *Farewell to Manzanar: A True Story of Japanese American Experience during and after the World War II Internment*. New York: Houghton Mifflin, 2002.

Isserman, Maurice. *World War II, Updated Edition*. America at War. New York: Facts On File, 2003.

Jackson, Kenneth T. *Crabgrass Frontier: The Suburbanization of the United States*. New York: Oxford University Press, 1987.

Leman, Nicholas. *The Promised Land: The Great Black Migration and How It Changed America*. New York: Vintage, 1992.

Lingeman, Richard R. *Don't You Know There's a War On? The American Home Front, 1941–1945*. New York: Richard R. Nation Books, 2003.

McKissack, Pat, and Fredrick L. McKissack. *Red-Tail Angels: The Story of the Tuskegee Airmen of World War II*. New York: Walker & Co., 2001.

Morris, Jan. *Manhattan '45*. New York: Oxford University Press, 1987.

Nathan, Amy. *Yankee Doodle Gal: Women Pilots of World War II*. Washington, D.C.: National Geographic, 2001.

Perret, Geoffrey. *Days of Sadness, Years of Triumph: The American People, 1939–45.* Madison: University of Wisconsin Press, 1985.

Powers, Ron. *Flags of Our Fathers: Heroes of Iwo Jima.* New York: Delacorte Books for Young Readers, 2003.

Robinson, Sharon. *Promises To Keep: How Jackie Robinson Changed America.* New York: Scholastic, 2004.

Ross, Stewart. *The Causes of the Cold War.* New York: World Almanac, 2002.

Stanley, George E. *Harry S. Truman: Thirty-Third President of the United States.* New York: Aladdin, 2004.

Tuttle, William M., Jr. *Daddy's Gone to War: The Second World War in the Lives of America's Children.* New York: Oxford University Press, 1995.

Uschan, Michael V., ed. *The 1940s.* Cultural History of the United States Through the Decades. San Diego: Lucent Books, 1999.

Weinstein, Allen. *Perjury: The Hiss-Chambers Case.* New York: Random House, 1997.

Whitman, Sylvia. *V Is for Victory: The American Home Front During World War II.* New York: Lerner Publications, 2002.

Winkler, Allan M. *Home Front U.S.A.: America During World War II.* Wheeling, Ill.: Harlan Davidson, 2000.

WEBSITES

CNN Perspectives. "Cold War," Available online. URL: www.cnn.com/SPECIALS/cold.war/. Downloaded in June 2005.

Dirks, Tim. "Film History of the 1940s," Available online. URL: www.filmsite.org/40sintro.html. Updated in 2005.

Early Television Museum. "Postwar Television," Available online. URL: http://www.early television.org. Updated on May 1, 2005.

History Place. "African-Americans in World War II," Available online. URL: www.historyplace. com/unitedstates/aframerwar/. Downloaded in June 2005.

Kingwood College Library. "American Cultural History, 1940s," Available online. URL: http://kclibrary.nhmccd.edu/decade40.html. Updated in May 2004.

Library of Congress American Memory. "Jackie Robinson," Available online. URL: http://lcweb2. loc.gov/ammem/collections/robinson/. Downloaded in June 2005.

National Archives. "A People at War," Available online. URL: www.archives.gov/exhibit_hall/a_people_at_war/a_people_at_war.html. Downloaded in June 2005.

National Atomic Museum. "Manhattan Project," Available online. URL: http://www.atomicmuseum.com/tour/manhattanproject.cfm. Downloaded in June 2005.

PBS. "American Experience: D-Day," Available online. http://www.pbs.org/wgbh/amex/dday/. Downloaded in June 2005.

PBS. "American Experience: Eleanor Roosevelt," Available online. URL: www.pbs.org/wgbh/amex/eleanor/. Downloaded in June 2005.

"Rosie the Riveter," Available online. URL: http://www.rosietheriveter.org/. Downloaded in June 2005.

Smithsonian Institution. "Japanese-American Internment," Available online. URL: http://americanhistory.si.edu/perfectunion/experience/index.html. Downloaded in June 2005.

White House. "Franklin D. Roosevelt," Available online. URL: http://www.whitehouse.gov/history/presidents/fr32.html. Downloaded in June 2005.

White House. "Harry Truman," Available online. URL: www.whitehouse.gov/history/presidents/ht33.html—Hollywood. Downloaded in June 2005.

INDEX

Page numbers in *italics* indicate illustrations. Page numbers followed by *g* indicate glossary entries. Page numbers in **boldface** indicate box features.